RED

RESCUE FROM ETERNAL DEATH

An Exposition of God's Gift of Salvation Suitable for Individual and Small Group Study

SEGUN DARAMOLA

RED: Rescue from Eternal Death

ISBN Paperback : 979-8-9914592-0-4

ISBN Hardcover: 979-8-9914592-1-1

ISBN Ebook: 979-8-9914592-2-8.

CONTENTS

INTRODUCTION

Every time I write something that relates to the Christian faith, whether I am writing in my daily devotion journal or in my prayer journal, or whether I am typing the words of a book as I am doing now, there's a pressure, a feeling of heaviness, a literal weight I always feel in my heart. The last thing I want to do is to present a thought, a perspective, or an opinion that is not based on scriptural and spiritual truth or to share words that only stir up people's emotions or lead them away from the conviction of the Spirit of God. No matter how hard or light that it hits, I want the foundation of these words to be the eternal, living, and active Word of God itself. I realize our world has moved and keeps moving further and further away from the truth of the Word of God, and even from the desire to hear it. It is becoming more difficult to live the truth of God's Word. If it is not the feeling of being out of place, it is the internal struggle within oneself to keep walking the path of righteousness, no matter how unpopular it has become, and one's own desire to want to do and live differently. I also experience feelings of inadequacy, knowing full well that if I were to be judged by the words I write, I'd fall short all the time, and that makes it very difficult to even try to write. I couldn't say who or what is the source of that feeling of inadequacy.

However, the beauty about all of this is that this feeling serves as the perfect backdrop for what this devotional guide is about. It is the very thing that speaks to the condemnation we feel, the guilt and shame we carry, until we encounter the One who has the power to free us from that burden. Life is messed up; I'm not sure about you, but there are days when I doubt if anything good will come out of this life we are living, when all is said and done. The depravity and dysfunction of the world are at an all-time high, and there are still heights it can reach. We are so disconnected and removed from the plan and purpose of God for our lives that we have become gods for and of ourselves. Whether by our own desire or by the pressure of the society we live in, reaching for the things of God—His purity, character, and holiness—is becoming more and more foreign. The need to fit in, to not be cancelled, to not lose what we erroneously believe to be valuable—all of this leads us to where we now find ourselves: living a life that is outside God's will, a life led by self, pride, arrogance, evil, hate, depravity, immorality, corruption, greed, idolatry, and ungodliness.

To make matters worse—and I am not really sure when this started or how it has evolved to this delusional and self-destructive perspective and attitude to God and to life—we have taken the love of God as a license to indulge in every kind of self-led and self-satisfying desire, making His love and grace into a shield against eternal consequences and condemnation, even when we knowingly and purposely decide to live in a way that leads to eternal condemnation and ultimate separation from God. We no longer want to ruffle feathers, ours and everyone else's, so our songs and teachings are filled with false encouragements and assertion of His mercy without us allowing it to lead us to repentance. We say sin does not matter anymore, that God understands, and that He has paid the price for it. Yes, He did, but is it supposed to end there? Was His death meant just to buy us a "sin for free" card? We have made room for our depravity in God's space, the place we have been invited to sit with Him, a place where there is strength and grace for every battle we face. Some of us do not accept His invitation and go our own way, and even the ones that do, want to do so based on their terms, still holding on to the things that His invitation is freeing us from.

This is our world and present construct, but in all of this craziness, the often ignored, overlooked, and despised solution to all that ails the world still exits, still calls us, still offers us and invites us to righteousness, purity, and truth, a life free of guilt and condemnation. God offers a life guaranteed with a daily supply of grace, counsel, leading, guidance, protection, peace, and prosperity of our soul foremost, and then everything else that needs prospering. We call this thing *salvation*, God's salvation, a change in spiritual location, an escape from the power and penalty of sin, and an exclusion from eternal death. God chose to offer this salvation through His Son, Jesus Christ, the only one who was worthy enough to carry the sins and rebellion of this world. He put that weight on His shoulders and paid the ultimate price for it: His life. That is what this book is about: understanding this precious gift in order that we might receive the full benefit of it and not abuse it.

Jesus answered, "I am the way and the truth and the life. No one comes to the Father except through me." (John 14:6)

Salvation is found in no one else, for there is no other name under heaven given to mankind by which we must be saved. (Acts 4:12)

I'd like to put these Scripture verses out there to remove any ambiguity or confusion regarding salvation, as this is what I believe. This is what the Word of God says: outside of Jesus Christ, eternal dwelling with God is impossible, the forgiveness of sin is not possible, and freedom from the penalty of sin will forever elude us. I understand this automatically puts the Christian faith in contention with other faiths and beliefs, but it is what it is. Jesus did not say this so that we can hate everybody else or be intolerant in society; it is a word spoken to everyone, even those who profess to be Christians. Whether or not you were born into a Christian home does not matter; at some point in your life, you will be faced with the decision to surrender your life to God and accept His salvation. It is a decision everyone must make regardless of faith, nationality, and race. Jesus is that door that we all need to decide to walk through. If we decide not to, that is fine as well, but understand that if the goal and desire is to spend eternity with God, then any other door will only lead to where God's glory is not and will never be.

These two Scripture verses form the basis of our devotion and study in the sessions to follow. Our desire is to understand what brought about salvation, what it is, what we need to do to get it, and what we must do with it once we get it. There are four sessions in this study, and each study session starts with engaging the mind and spirit with questions that help to focus on what the session will be about. After every session is an opportunity to pray, and this is not only to help us understand that Scripture reveals our inability, but it also helps us realize our dependency on God. One of the most effective and fulfilling ways to engage in prayer is to use the Word of God as a guide to communicate back to God, as this guarantees that we are not only praying with understanding but also praying in accordance with His will.

I pray that as you go through this book, the Spirit of God will open your eyes and your heart to see and perceive the wonder of His love as well as this great work He has done on our behalf and in our place. I pray that conviction will rise in your heart to accept Him if you have not yet done so, and if you have, that a greater appreciation will arise in you for the salvation that you have received. Be blessed as you read!

SESSION 1

SIN IS THE REASON

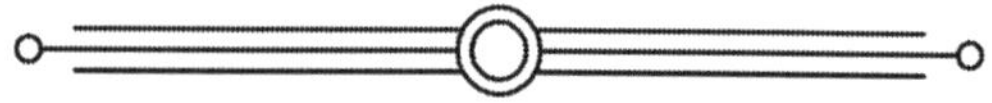

Surely the arm of the Lord is
not too short to save,
nor his ear too dull to hear.
But your iniquities have
separated
you from your God;
your sins have hidden his face
from you,
so that he will not hear.

(Isaiah 59:1–2)

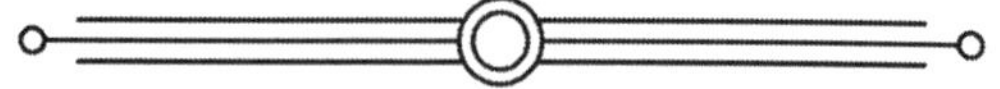

INTRODUCTION

In this session, we want to lay a very important foundation, which is to understand why it became necessary for God to make for us a way of salvation. The lack of understanding is pretty glaring in our world, and even in the church quite a few of us do not truly grasp or are able to fully comprehend the need to surrender one's life to Christ and be saved. Not understanding what brought about our need to be saved makes us think this is either an unnecessary step or a completely optional decision we need to make. This study will take us back to the very beginning, and we will work our way to the point where the need for salvation became apparent. As we do so, hopefully our eyes, ears, and hearts will be opened to receive and accept what God will reveal to us by His Spirit.

ICEBREAKER

Imagine experiencing a break in a relationship in your life (maybe some of you actually have). Then imagine that at some point later, an opportunity opened for you and the person you were in a relationship with to sit down and work at reconciliation and recommitment. How possible will this reconciliation be if you suddenly realized midway through your conversation that you are not both on the same page as to why the relationship was broken or disrupted in the first place?

GUARDRAIL OR RESTRICTION?

Most of the vacations I have taken in my lifetime have been at some beach. I think one of the most refreshing scenes for the mind and the soul is the glory of a huge expanse of water. One thing I like to do if I get the chance is to stand by the shore during sunset and look straight ahead as far as my eyes can see, deep into the ocean, to the point where it feels like the sky meets the sea. There is an orange shadow that the sun leaves behind as it bids one side of the world goodbye. I would stare in amazement and awe at it, wondering what it would be like if that was a place that I could experience without being consumed by its glory. It makes one feel kind of small, doesn't it?

Personally, I don't get too deep into the water; I prefer to do all my swimming in a pool! But let's say you were at a beach, and in a particular section, you saw a sign that read something like this:

How would you interpret this? What goes through your mind? Fear, curiosity, uncertainty, intrigue? You need to decide either to adhere to the rule and turn back or to ignore and proceed. What would you do? It all depends on how you interpret this. To some, this may mean that someone was kind enough to be looking out for them, that there is danger on the other side, and that someone loves them enough to not want to see them get hurt. These people see this sign and obey what is on it; they turn back. To them, this sign is a guardrail.

To others, this sign means someone does not want them to experience the fullness of what the ocean has to offer; someone is trying to tell them what to do or infringe on their freedom. Even if they might acknowledge there may be danger, they are pretty confident they can take care of themselves; better still, they think there probably is no danger on the other side, and the allure of the experience ahead is too much to pass up, so they ignore the sign and proceed. To these people, this sign is a restriction.

As simple as this illustration is, it is really the cornerstone of our war and battle with God from the very beginning up until now. How we interpret God's intention and purpose toward us is the deciding factor of our commitment to Him or lack thereof. This issue showed itself at the very first occurrence of man's rebellion against God. We will jump into that study in a minute, but before that, here is an opportunity for meditation, discussion, or both.

››› THINK AND TALK ABOUT IT ‹‹‹

Are there moments in your life for which you have had to decide if God's instruction to you was a guardrail or restriction? How did knowing or not knowing what was beyond the instruction affect your response to Him? If you were to put one of these two words to your general attitude and disposition to the Word of God, what would it be?

I personally think if one can understand and comprehend what went on in Genesis 3, then one has attained complete mastery of the state of our world and what drives its dysfunction. Let us study a few verses and see what we can learn.

Now the serpent was more crafty than any of the wild animals the LORD God had made. He said to the woman, "Did God really say, 'You must not eat from any tree in the garden'?"

The woman said to the serpent, "We may eat fruit from the trees in the garden, but God did say, 'You must not eat fruit from the tree that is in the middle of the garden, and you must not touch it, or you will die.' "

"You will not certainly die," the serpent said to the woman. "For God knows that when you eat from it your eyes will be opened, and you will be like God, knowing good and evil."

When the woman saw that the fruit of the tree was good for food and pleasing to the eye, and also desirable for gaining wisdom, she took some and ate it. She also gave some to her husband, who was with her, and he ate it. Then the eyes of both of them were opened, and they realized they were naked; so they sewed fig leaves together and made coverings for themselves.
(Genesis 3:1–7)

Let us talk about this Scripture passage in light of these three points.

1. WHEN THE INTENTION OF GOD IS DOUBTED, THE TEMPTATION TO WALK AWAY COMES NEXT.

I am not about to go into some kind of theological soliloquy on what God said, what He did not say, was He misquoted or misinterpreted, did the devil lie, what exactly did he lie about, did Adam give Eve the full story, and if not, why not, and so on. There is just one simple thing to ask: If someone gave you an instruction, and someone else came to attempt to alter or discredit the instruction, I would think the first logical thing to do would be to go back to the one who gave the instruction and question his or her integrity to their face. Unless this did happen and it is hidden from us, it is amazing to me that Adam and Eve did not even think to go back to God to clarify or even question His intention based on what the devil said. There is nothing wrong in questioning what God's plan and purpose is for your life. However, the devil's game plan is not for you to go back to God for clarification or a strengthening of your faith; it is for you to doubt and walk away from God's presence. The devil knows he cannot get you to sin in God's presence, when your faith is close to its source, but he invites you to wander away. He gives you an invitation that lures you away into an attempt to discover something better than what God has given you.

> **The LORD God took the man and put him in the Garden of Eden to work it and take care of it. And the LORD God commanded the man, "You are free to eat from any tree in the garden; but you must not eat from the tree of the knowledge of good and evil, for when you eat from it you will certainly die." (Genesis 2:15–17)**

Unfortunately, Adam and Eve saw this command as a restriction instead of a guardrail, and they were convinced and deceived to think that God did not have their best in mind. From this point, walking away became easy. I also think it is not too far-fetched to think that this doubt had been building up for a while. The devil did not have to put in too much work, or at least so it seems.

››› THINK AND TALK ABOUT IT ‹‹‹

Why would God lie to you? What would He have to gain?

2. THE EYE CANNOT SIN WHERE THE HEART HAS NOT FIRST CONCEIVED.

But each person is tempted when they are dragged away by their own evil desire and enticed. (James 1:14)

The apostle James makes us understand that sin starts when our desires begin to lead us away from truth. Our desires, not anyone else's. Yes, we get pressured by friends, society, and the world, but ultimately, we don't move until our desires start to lead us. We ask ourselves, Did the devil really sow a seed of doubt, or did he fan into flames something that was already in Adam and Eve's heart? The heart is the powerhouse of all desires, and it's no surprise that Solomon said this in the book of Proverbs.

Above all else, guard your heart, for everything you do flows from it. (Proverbs 4:23)

Was there something in the hearts of Adam and Eve that they desired but that God did not want them to have? Was this thing important enough to make them disobey God and do the very thing He said not to do? What must have gotten into them? How could they think there was a better plan than the one God had for them? I am not expecting an answer to these questions; rather, I want to use them as a starting point for looking inward and assessing our desires and what goes on in our hearts when we disobey God and choose to live a life outside of His commands. With all that is available for our hearts to consume these days, it's no surprise some of us are struggling with accepting God's plan and purpose. We have fed ourselves with so much anti-God stuff that every desire in us is no longer for him. The desire for the things of God do not come naturally, and so if all we feed on builds in us ungodly wants and desires, we naturally would do ungodly things.

It amazes me how the devil and man were in sync and aligned in their thought process. There were two trees in the middle of the garden. God never said not to eat from the tree of life. So how did Eve know exactly which tree the devil was referring to, and how did the devil know Eve was referring to the tree of the knowledge of good and evil when she did not mention the name directly? I say all that to say this: If you find yourself in one sin or the other, be honest with yourself and assess your desires.

››› THINK AND TALK ABOUT IT ‹‹‹

How has the world around you affected the guardrails around your heart? What temps you to let down your guard?

3. THE NEED TO BE IN CONTROL PUSHES GOD OFF THE THRONE.

If the devil came out and said, "Come, let me be your god," I am pretty sure that most of us would say, "Thanks, but no thanks." But what if he said, "You know, you don't need anyone telling you what to do; you can be your own god," this sounds different, and we might be more receptive to the invitation. If you think this is strange, you only need to look at Adam and Eve again.

When the woman saw that the fruit of the tree was good for food and pleasing to the eye, and also desirable for gaining wisdom, she took some and ate it. She also gave some to her husband, who was with her, and he ate it. (Genesis 3:6)

Eve saw that the fruit was good for food, and she did see right, because every fruit that God made was good for food. She saw the fruit was pleasing to the eye, and once again she saw right, for God did make every fruit pleasing to the eye.

The LORD God made all kinds of trees grow out of the ground—trees that were pleasing to the eye and good for food. In the middle of the garden were the tree of life and the tree of the knowledge of good and evil. (Genesis 2:9)

If the tree was good and pleasing to the eye, then the fruit was good and pleasing to the eye. So what exactly is the problem here? What caused Adam and Eve's downfall; what drove them to disobey God? Well, what you will not find in any of the creation accounts is that God made something that could give man wisdom. Why would He? Why did they need wisdom when they could get all their instructions and wisdom from God? They were created in God's image, and in order to maintain that image, they would have to live in obedience and total surrender. But the allure of being in control, to determine what is right and wrong for oneself (this ought to sound eerily familiar), and to call the shots for themselves was too strong for them to pass up. They wanted to be in charge. Moreover, as you can see in the Scripture verses below, the devil did actually tell them something that was true, albeit deceptive.

And the LORD God said, "The man has now become like one of us, knowing good and evil." (Genesis 3:22a)

Look at the devil's words earlier!

For God knows that when you eat from it your eyes will be opened, and you will be like God, knowing good and evil. (Genesis 3:5)

This really is the crux of the matter: the need for control, the allure of self-governance, the ability to be in charge of one's own desire and appetite. To do what one wants to do when one wants to do it: this is the inception and conception of sin; this is what drives us to the edge. This is the lie Adam and Eve were sold, and unfortunately this is the lie that many of us are still buying and accepting. We want to be in control of our lives and do as we please, but this is sin. This was and is still our downfall. Every other thing we do wrong in life is the fruit of subverting God's authority over our lives and directing the course of our lives ourselves.

››› THINK AND TALK ABOUT IT ‹‹‹

How easy or difficult of a process has it been for you to give God full control? Do you ever feel the need to take that control back and navigate life by yourself?

ETERNAL CONSEQUENCE

It may surprise you to know that the impact of sin is the same, whether we are in relationship with God or not. Sin leads us away from God, and the more we live in it, the further it takes us away from God.

We all, like sheep, have gone astray, each of us has turned to our own way. (Isaiah 53:6a)

For those who do not believe, sin keeps them away, and for those who believe and continue to sin, it leads them astray and away. The ultimate goal of sin is to lead us into eternal separation. There is so much confusion on this subject even in the Christian community. Some people believe that the moment you are born again, sin can no longer damage your relationship with God, even if you keep living in sin. This is so far from the truth! I encourage us not to believe this lie and to keep sin at bay by the grace that God gives. The devil is still at work, and he has not given up trying to discredit the work of salvation to make sure we do not reap the ultimate benefit. Do not be deceived; something breaks when we sin. Things start to change the moment we decide to start playing god in our own lives.

So the LORD God banished him from the Garden of Eden to work the ground from which he had been taken. After he drove the man out, he placed on the east side of the Garden of Eden cherubim and a flaming sword flashing back and forth to guard the way to the tree of life. (Genesis 3:23–24)

There are two things I feel we can learn from what happened here. As hard as it is to comprehend, the first thing that jumps out is the fact that God Himself kicked Adam and Eve out of the Garden. I think this is because it is not possible for us to live in sin and in God's purpose at the same time. Our current state will determine where we are. If we choose sin, then we can't be in His plan and purpose. It's just that simple. I also understand that while we are walking through this life, we fall here and there and every now and then, but this fact will help you understand the redemptive power in the blood of Jesus and how quickly it brings us back in line when we confess and acknowledge our sins. We will get into that later.

When we get kicked out of God's purpose and plan, it does not mean that life falls apart or that we no longer have material prosperity or success. It does not mean you will no longer get promoted or get opportunities. Actually, this is also where a lot of people miss the point; they feel that because they are prospering and things are working, it must mean that God is with and for them and that the life of sin they are living does not matter. This is a huge misconception, because if the only way to prosper on this earth is to stop sinning and believe in God, then the only people who would be rich, wealthy, and successful here on earth would be Christians, and you and I know that this is not the case. Yes, ultimately God is the source of all blessing and favor, but there is a difference between God prospering you and God letting you prosper—a big difference! God does not use money or wealth to force people into His Kingdom. As much as the experiences of the children of Israel and the commandments they received may make you think that there is a direct correlation between sin and wealth, I would advise you to go back and study the Old Testament and get a good understanding of the context. There were other nations who were worshipping idols and living in disobedience but still prospering. God wanted to be the source for the children of Israel's prosperity, but if they kept sinning, God was not going to prosper or protect them from their enemies, who wanted to take all they had.

Take a look at David's prayer in Psalm 51:

Do not cast me from your presence or take your Holy Spirit from me. (Psalm 51:11)

Another way to think about this is that sin forces God to do what He would not want to do as a Father, but because He has to honor His word above His name, at some point He lets go and gives us over to the sin that we do not want to leave alone. Why would He do that? God is holy, and He will not align Himself with unholiness. He forgives sin, but sin will not define or redefine God. He separates Himself from anything unholy or ungodly. When we make the decision not to leave sin alone, He will make the decision to move us out of His presence so nothing unholy dwells in His presence. We can say this in so many ways, but I hope the message is clear and that we do not appear to be abusing the grace of God and neglecting the impact that sin can have in our lives.

The second thing we can learn is that Adam and Eve were barred from the tree of life, as God specifically said in the Scripture verse below:

He must not be allowed to reach out his hand and take also from the tree of life and eat, and live forever. (Genesis 3:22b)

Sin will ultimately deprive us of the eternal life we have been promised, the life that we will live with Him once this temporary existence is over. As much as the devil wants to cause us pain and grief here on earth, and to make us question God's goodness to us, what he really wants is for us to be separated from God completely and for all eternity. He already knows his end and the punishment that awaits, and he wants to make sure that he does not end up there alone. He wants to deceive as many as he can, and sin is the method through which he deceives.

Then, after desire has conceived, it gives birth to sin; and sin, when it is full-grown, gives birth to death. (James 1:15)

We are not referring simply to the individual error of our ways; we are talking about the ideology and motive behind the life we live. The only way something can fully grow is if you keep nurturing it, and the only way sin is fully nurtured is if it has become our way of life and ideology. This will ultimately lead to death and eternal separation from God.

THIS IS WHY

Based on what we have talked about so far, let us take a few moments to meditate on the Scripture passage below and see if it takes on a whole new meaning or reaffirms your understanding of it before now. The emphasis is on verse 9, but it is good to read the surrounding Scripture verses so we can lay a good contextual background.

> **Everyone who sins breaks the law; in fact, sin is lawlessness. But you know that he appeared so that he might take away our sins. And in him is no sin. No one who lives in him keeps on sinning. No one who continues to sin has either seen him or known him. Dear children, do not let anyone lead you astray. The one who does what is right is righteous, just as he is righteous. The one who does what is sinful is of the devil, because the devil has been sinning from the beginning. The reason the Son of God appeared was to destroy the devil's work. No one who is born of God will continue to sin, because God's seed remains in them; they cannot go on sinning, because they have been born of God. This is how we know who the children of God are and who the children of the devil are: Anyone who does not do what is right is not God's child, nor is anyone who does not love their brother and sister. (1 John 3:4–10)**

Jesus came to destroy the devil's work, and the devil's work is sin; it is that simple. Jesus did not come to secure your 401k and help you hedge your losses in the stock market. I am not saying that He cannot give you the wisdom to do that, but if that is all He came for, then I think being hung up on the cross and experiencing death is a bit of an overkill, don't you think? Leaving behind glory, subjecting Himself to the torture of the earthly vessel He had to live in, daily temptation, and the excruciating pain He endured to secure our release from death was not just for some fancy lifestyle, beautiful clothes, and fast cars (and boy, do I love fast cars!). It is more than that: if He did not come, sin would still have us. It is still trying to have us every day. The devil is still working to make sure we miss God's salvation eternally and experience eternal darkness and condemnation with him. This is why Jesus came—this is the reason, the only reason!

As much as it hurts to say it, this reason has been lost in the Christian world and most especially the church. In the bid to attract people to the pews and stay in the good graces of the secular world, the messaging has shifted from a focus on sin and Christ to a self-focus. The average church message paints you as this victim who has gone through so much and to whom God owes so much. They say God is so desperate to be loved by you that you need do nothing and He does everything; you don't need to change your life; He's paid for all your sins, so feel free to keep on sinning; you see, it is not about what we do, because God loves us regardless. Unfortunately, this is the most erroneous interpretation and understanding of the love of God, but this is what people are comfortable with now. This is what they want to hear, because the pull and allure of the life we all want to live so arrogantly and deceitfully is stronger than our desire to long after righteousness. Hope is not lost, however, because for as long as we are here, it is never too late to return to true righteousness and worship. We must keep sin in focus not to be condemned by it but as people who have been made victorious. By God's wisdom, we have figured out the schemes of the enemy, but we must ensure we are no longer deceived and must always be mindful of how he still wants to trap us and destroy us, knowing fully well that God has given us power over sin.

As we prayerfully wrap up this session and approach the next, I would like for us to ponder on all that we have discussed, taking time to meditate on the Scripture passages we examined. Use the prayers below as a guide to have a conversation with God, asking Him for grace and help in the areas where we need it. Don't forget to celebrate the fact that He did not leave us under the defeat of sin; He loved us enough to make a way out for us.

››› PRAYER OPPORTUNITIES AND FOCUS ‹‹‹

- *In the early part of the session, we talked about doubting God's goodness and intentions toward us and how this always opened a door for sin to creep in. Are there still doubts in your mind about who God says He is? I am not talking about the doubt of whether He will decide to do something or give something; I am referring to the doubt that questions His existence, love, and authority over your life. This will be a great opportunity to take this doubt to Him in prayer. This is a very important conversation to have, so be open and honest about it. Be vulnerable enough to voice your doubts and ask for His help, for assurance to come, for your hope to be strengthened, and for Him to reveal Himself and speak to you by His Spirit.*
- *The worst thing that could ever happen is for us to live in sin or be under the power and hold of sin but to live in denial, excuse it, or explain it away. Forgiveness and redemption will never come if there is no acknowledgment of our fallen state. We have an opportunity right now to go before God and*

acknowledge our sins and shortcomings. Not that He does not know where we are, but the love of God will not confess our sins for us or repent for us; it can only lead us to the point where we need to do these things. That love is with you right now, so go ahead and do what needs to be done.

SESSION 2

THIS THING CALLED SALVATION

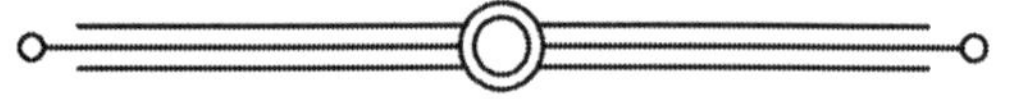

For God did not appoint us to suffer wrath but to receive salvation through our Lord Jesus Christ.

(1 Thessalonians 5:9)

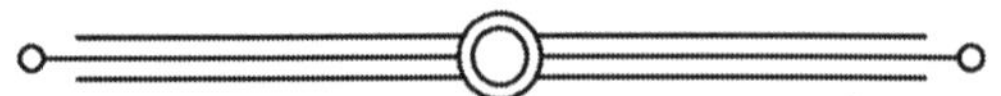

INTRODUCTION

I hope that we laid a very good foundation in the preceding session, one that will help us appreciate what we are about to get into in this session. Sin is the enemy, and salvation in Christ is at the core of redemption, the escape that God has provided and freely offered to as many as are willing to accept it. We want to dig deeper into this, the price that was paid for our sin. Through whom do we access it, and what does it do for us once we receive it? This is a core belief, that we are unable and incapable of saving ourselves, and we need salvation and a Savior.

ICEBREAKER

Does sin give you a sense of hopelessness? How have you navigated those moments? Have you ever had to rescue someone from some kind of danger, or have you been rescued by someone? If you have been a rescuer, what drove you to rescue, and if you have been rescued, what was going through your mind as you were being rescued?

WHAT MUST GIVE?

> **God presented Christ as a sacrifice of atonement, through the shedding of his blood—to be received by faith. He did this to demonstrate his righteousness, because in his forbearance he had left the sins committed beforehand unpunished. (Romans 3:25)**

The job of a lifeguard is very important. It demands a great deal of skill, especially when it comes to performing one of the most crucial responsibilities of the job: rescuing and saving someone who is in distress and unable to save themselves. Certification classes in various rescue and lifesaving techniques are a fundamental requirement for a person to be designated as a lifesaver. Victim rescue, ability to give CPR, administering oxygen in emergency situations—these are just a few of the skills a lifeguard needs to have. In essence, a lifeguard knows what to do and how to save someone in distress. However, it is not beyond humanity's arrogance and lack of understanding for someone in distress in the water to try to instruct the lifeguard on how he or she should be rescued. Sounds crazy, right? In order to be rescued, the one in distress must trust and completely yield to the one who is doing the rescuing. If you could save yourself, then you would not need a lifeguard, would you?

Why is this important when it comes to salvation? Well, since our sins have caused a separation between us and God, in order for there to be reconciliation and restoration, the terms of engagement cannot come from the offender but must come from the one who was offended. It is impossible for us to truly appreciate the full impact of our sins from our own point view. It is God who sees and knows our sins. He is the one who sees the true separation it causes. Since that is the case, then He is the one who knows what needs to be done for redemption and restoration to occur; it cannot be us. We will need to accept salvation on His terms and not ours. He gets to choose how we must be saved. He is the lifeguard, and when He wants to pull us out of the water of sin and depravity, we cannot tell Him how to do it, when He should do it, and what He needs to use to do it.

The experience of the children of Israel in Numbers 21 should help us understand this a bit more.

> **They traveled from Mount Hor along the route to the Red Sea, to go around Edom. But the people grew impatient on the way; they spoke against God and against Moses, and said, "Why have you brought us up out of Egypt to die in the wilderness? There is no bread! There is no water! And we detest this miserable food!"**
>
> **Then the LORD sent venomous snakes among them; they bit the people and many Israelites died. The people came to Moses and said, "We sinned when we spoke against the LORD and against you. Pray that the LORD will take the snakes away from us." So Moses prayed for the people. The LORD said to Moses, "Make a snake and put it up on a pole; anyone who is bitten can look at it and live." So Moses made a bronze snake and put it up on a pole. Then when anyone was bitten by a snake and looked at the bronze snake, they lived. (Numbers 21:4–9)**

I hope you see the pattern here. The children of Israel sinned against God, and there was a consequence for that. They found themselves in distress, and so they cried out to God. Then God gave instructions as to how they could escape the consequence of their sin. Salvation came from God and not from them. I will be using this passage of Scripture later in this session to make another point that relates to what has just been said, so keep this in your heart for now.

Even though the Scripture passage below does not directly relate to salvation, I include this here to point out the human arrogance and stubbornness I mentioned earlier, when sometimes we try to dictate to God how things should be done.

> **So Naaman went with his horses and chariots and stopped at the door of Elisha's house. Elisha sent a messenger to say to him, "Go, wash yourself seven times in the Jordan, and your flesh will be restored and you will be cleansed."**
>
> **But Naaman went away angry and said, "I thought that he would surely come out to me and stand and call on the name of the LORD his God, wave his hand over the spot and cure me of my leprosy. Are not Abana and Pharpar, the rivers of Damascus, better than all the waters of Israel? Couldn't I wash in them and be cleansed?" So he turned and went off in a rage. (2 Kings 5:9–12)**

I hope you see the pattern here as well. This man called Naaman had leprosy, and he had been sent to Elisha the prophet to be healed. Elisha gave an instruction, but Naaman got upset because the manner in which his healing was going to come did not align with his own expectation. He had better ideas. It is amazing, isn't it? The one who is helpless is trying to tell the one who is willing to help how he must go about helping. It is simply arrogance.

The salvation we are discussing here is not something that we have made up ourselves. It is not a pathway to God created by humans, a set of rules and regulations (or the lack thereof) published by some religious body to get back into God's good graces, and it is certainly not a concept derived for the purpose of entertaining and accommodating man's desire to live in sin and rebellion. This is God's way, His prescribed method, what He wrote in His Word. It is what He has passed down to us and what we must also pass along to others.

> **Jesus is "the stone you builders rejected, which has become the cornerstone." Salvation is found in no one else, for there is no other name under heaven given to mankind by which we must be saved. (Acts 4:11–12)**

> **But now apart from the law the righteousness of God has been made known, to which the Law and the Prophets testify. This righteousness is given through faith in Jesus Christ to all who believe. There is no difference between Jew and Gentile, for all have sinned and fall short of the glory of God, and all are justified freely by his grace through the redemption that came by Christ Jesus. (Romans 3:21–24)**

The Word of God is explicit when it says that Jesus is the gateway to salvation and redemption. We are going to have to believe it or not believe it. He was the only one qualified to offer Himself to save us. We can get into all sorts of theological explanations for why He is—some of which we will get into later on. But after every Bible study, every breakdown of the Word, every exegesis, it always boils down to one question, and the question is this: Do you believe? Are you willing for your faith to accept this and use this as fuel for your life's journey? That is a question only you can answer and a decision only you can make.

››› THINK AND TALK ABOUT IT ‹‹‹

Have you ever struggled with the truth of Scripture concerning God's way of salvation?

THIS IS HOW HE DID IT

> **When you were dead in your sins and in the uncircumcision of your flesh, God made you alive with Christ. He forgave us all our sins, having canceled the charge of our legal indebtedness, which stood against us and condemned us; he has taken it away, nailing it to the cross. And having disarmed the powers and authorities, he made a public spectacle of them, triumphing over them by the cross. (Colossians 2:13–15)**

We are going to forget about ourselves for a little while. What I mean is this: we are going to lay aside what we need to do to be saved and focus solely on what God did to make salvation available, and what became available as a result of what He did. Once we gain that understanding, we will shift the focus back to us. Salvation is made possible as a result of God's loving and merciful nature. He gives us His love and mercy even while we are in our sins, which is not a natural response. He does so through the salvation won by His Son, Jesus.

> **For the wages of sin is death, but the gift of God is eternal life in Christ Jesus our Lord. (Romans 6:23)**

What sin deserves is a penalty, and that penalty is death. God warned Adam that the consequence of his sin would be death, and surely when he sinned, he died: the purity of his relationship with God died. A distance and a gulf was created between him and God as a result of his sin. He lost his place before God, and God had no choice but to put him out to serve the master to which he had now surrendered himself. For as long as sin was in play, man was under the rule and the authority of the penalty of sin, which is death.

It still holds true today: until a man or woman surrenders their life to Jesus Christ, they are still under the reign and rule of sin's penalty, no matter how good or morally upright they may seem to be. Salvation is a gift, given solely at the discretion and disposition of the giver. You can't and must never look at yourself and say, "I deserved to be saved," or "God had no choice but to save me." Oh, yes, He did have a choice. He could have turned the other way. He could have left us to our own devices and created something else to love and have fellowship with. We did not deserve to be saved. The relationship you are enjoying right now is a graceful and gracious life, and you must never forget that.

When we think of salvation, it is good to look at it from three distinct points: Christ's death, His descent into the grave, and His resurrection out of the grave. Here is an analogy that I think could help bring more light on this subject. When there is war between two countries and people or soldiers have been captured and need to be rescued, it will entail getting boots on the ground in the enemy territory. You would have to locate where the captives are being held, put a special team together, and figure out a way to break them out. There is a high possibility that you have to engage the enemy, because they will not voluntarily surrender anyone in their captivity.

Likewise, seeing that sin held us prisoner in the grave (in death), Jesus had to die and descend into the grave in order to break us free and bring us out. Did He face opposition? I believe He did, or else the Bible would not have told us that He triumphed. You don't triumph over something or someone if no battle ensued between you and the enemy. With His victory, we now live free, unashamed and without guilt.

I like the way Paul organized his message in Colossians 2:13–15.

Let's take a deeper dive into this text, studying for more clarity and meaning to what we have said so far. As we do, I pray you develop a more profound appreciation of God's love for you and this gift that you have received by putting your faith and trust in Jesus. If you have not done that, I pray that you will be convicted to do so today, knowing fully well that His invitation is open to all, and He eagerly awaits your decision.

There are two important things we can learn from Colossians 2:13–15 as it relates to salvation.

1. SIN IS FORGIVEN.

> **When you were dead in your sins and in the uncircumcision of your flesh, God made you alive with Christ. He forgave us all our sins. (Colossians 2:13)**

If sin caused the divide, then it would only make sense that this is the first thing to be addressed. This is why we spent the time we did in the first session talking about sin, not just seeing the fruit it cultivates but also considering the very root of it. For this relationship to be restored, God has to forgive us first of our rebellion—thinking we could be our own gods and taking Him off the throne of our lives—as well as every fruit that this rebellion has borne.

> **I am writing to you, dear children, because your sins have been forgiven on account of his name. (1 John 2:12)**

What does it mean to forgive? I checked Webster's dictionary and found a couple of interesting and relevant meanings. According to Webster, to *forgive* means to cease to feel resentment against an offender. It also means to give up resentment of or claim to requital or to grant relief to someone from payment of a debt. When someone offends you, you have the right to feel upset and be resentful of the person, but when you give up the feeling of resentment, that is forgiveness. Maybe that person deserved a certain reaction, and rightfully so; they should reap the consequences of their action, but you decide not to pay evil for evil or have them bear the consequences of their action. That is forgiveness.

I, even I, am he who blots out your transgressions, for my own sake, and remembers your sins no more. (Isaiah 43:25)

God looked at us and decided not to have us pay for our rebellion. He gave up His wrath and indignation toward us and instead poured out love and compassion. He went a step further by saying that the sins He has forgiven will no longer have a bearing on His relationship with us. I think that is what God meant when He said, "I will remember your sins no more." I find it hard to believe that God is forgetful. He knows everything and never forgets a thing. What He is telling us is that our sin will no longer be a thing between us and Him.

This is love: not that we loved God, but that he loved us and sent his Son as an atoning sacrifice for our sins. (1 John 4:10)

Before Jesus came, the burden of forgiveness was on the offender. It was the offender who needed to come forward with a sacrifice, bringing it before God to be forgiven. Now that is no longer the case: the sacrifice that brought about our forgiveness did not come from us; it came from God. He provided the Lamb that was worthy to be crucified, whose blood could truly wash sins away and offer complete release and deliverance from the penalty of sin.

> **All of us also lived among them at one time, gratifying the cravings of our flesh and following its desires and thoughts. Like the rest, we were by nature deserving of wrath. But because of his great love for us, God, who is rich in mercy, made us alive with Christ even when we were dead in transgressions—it is by grace you have been saved. (Ephesians 2:3–5)**

Let's say someone stole money from you, and that person asked to be forgiven, and you forgave them. To take it a step further, you do not require restitution from them; he or she does not have to return the stolen money. You no longer consider it a debt; you cut your losses and walk away. And with all that, your relationship with this person does not deteriorate; instead, there is actually opportunity for a true and meaningful relationship in spite of what transpired. That is forgiveness. This is hard to comprehend from a human standpoint, but this is forgiveness, God's forgiveness. Forgiveness with God means that He cancels the charge against us, and we no longer qualify for what sin would have brought our way had we not been saved.

››› THINK AND TALK ABOUT IT ‹‹‹

How can you use any of the things we have said about forgiveness to fight off the guilt and shame of the life you used to live before God saved you? If you have not yet given your life to Christ, does this help in any way to give you assurance that it is safe to come to God?

Let's turn back now to our second point from Colossians 2.

2. THERE IS VICTORY OVER SIN AND DEATH.

And having disarmed the powers and authorities, he made a public spectacle of them, triumphing over them by the cross. (Colossians 2:15)

Have you ever witnessed a court case where the defense attorney puts up such an excellent defense that the prosecution's case just falls apart, and every evidence is made so insignificant that there is no other choice but to dismiss the charges or find the defendant not guilty? The American judicial system has always been fascinating to me, especially the fact that someone accused of a crime can walk out of the courtroom free not necessarily because they are innocent but because the prosecution was not able to prove their guilt beyond a reasonable doubt. There is always the presumption of innocence before a trial, but is it not amazing that the jury verdict never contains the word *innocent* when it is read, and the defendant is found not guilty of whatever he or she has been accused of? The presumption of innocence before a trial remains a presumption of innocence after the trial if the defendant is found not guilty, because the jury verdict never declares him or her innocent.

I am in no way advocating for guilty people to go unpunished, but I do see some elements of this system in salvation's story. Let's dive in and talk about it.

> **Don't you know that when you offer yourselves to someone as obedient slaves, you are slaves of the one you obey—whether you are slaves to sin, which leads to death, or to obedience, which leads to righteousness? (Romans 6:16)**

When we live a life of sin, we are invariably ceding control of our lives to sin; we are under the control of sin. If we are under the control of sin, then our lives will ultimately be handed over to eternal death. When you are expecting a guest in your home, you prepare a room for them to stay. In the same way, death is preparing a place for everyone who is living in sin and refuses to turn around while they still have the opportunity. James helps us understand that death is the destination for the sinner (James 1:14–15). To death, its ownership over the sinner is legal and binding, and sin is what death presents as evidence when it is stating probable cause as to why it owns anyone living in sin. This is what makes Colossians 2:14 so relevant. God canceled the charge against us; however, it was a legal charge. We were not victims being treated unfairly or discriminated against; what we had coming, we deserved. This is a topic for another day, but if you listen to messages coming out of quite a number of churches nowadays, there is a tendency to over-victimize the listener to the point where folks no longer take responsibility for their actions. They feel nothing is wrong with them but that everything is wrong with everyone else, even when it comes to sin.

How then did God cancel this charge? Think about it: the wages of sin or the ultimate destination of a sinner is death, but when a man or woman sins, they do not sin against death; their sin is against God. If sin is against God, then God is the one who inputs the charge and not death. Death takes advantage of the charge, and claims ownership of the sinner because sin lives in the sinner and you cannot separate sin from death. Wherever sin is, death is lurking in the corner. But if God forgave the sin and the charge is removed (remember how we defined forgiveness earlier), then death has no case or probable cause to lay claim over the sinner. This is what Paul meant when he said God disarmed principalities and made a public spectacle of them (Colossians 2:15). Now that the most damming evidence has been thrown out, and the key witness is no longer willing to testify to support the prosecution's case, there is nothing to base conviction on. So, there is no other choice but to render the not guilty verdict. The defendant is free to go, not because he or she has not sinned, but because death can no longer prove its case beyond a reasonable doubt, death has surely lost its sting. Take a look at the Scripture passage below.

> **Then he showed me Joshua the high priest standing before the angel of the LORD, and Satan standing at his right side to accuse him. The LORD said to Satan, "The LORD rebuke you, Satan! The LORD, who has chosen Jerusalem, rebuke you! Is not this man a burning stick snatched from the fire?"**
>
> **Now Joshua was dressed in filthy clothes as he stood before the angel. The angel said to those who were standing before him, "Take off his filthy clothes." Then he said to Joshua, "See, I have taken away your sin, and I will put fine garments on you."**
>
> **(Zechariah 3:1–4)**

God discounts Satan's accusation against Joshua, forgives Joshua of his sins, and removes the charge against him. There is absolutely nothing that Satan can do after God does this. The moment God forgives Joshua, every accusation is meaningless. What makes this more beautiful is that God made intercession for Joshua by sympathizing with him, understanding where he was, and making a way out for him. This is the ultimate victory of salvation, that a man who is guilty of an offense can be forgiven and be allowed to walk out of the courtroom free, as if he had no guilt to begin with.

››› THINK AND TALK ABOUT IT ‹‹‹

Are you experiencing the victory of salvation? Are you able to share this experience with others?

THE CROSS AND THE BLOOD

> **"He himself bore our sins" in his body on the cross, so that we might die to sins and live for righteousness; "by his wounds you have been healed." (1 Peter 2:24)**

I feel the need to talk about the cross and the blood that was shed on it for a bit before we move on to the final part of this session. I believe that we can attach some significance to it that will be very helpful throughout our Christian journey, not only to help us remember what God did but also to serve as a revival and restoration point for times when things get a little (or a lot) out of control and we need to regain our footing in the journey. Jesus only died once; it was a once-and-for-all sacrifice. However, that does not mean we cannot return to this point every now and then as we feel the need. Based on where you and I are in life, here are some very critical points to take to heart and remember.

1. THE CROSS IS A PLACE OF SEPARATION.

> **From noon until three in the afternoon darkness came over all the land. About three in the afternoon Jesus cried out in a loud voice, "Eli, Eli, lema sabachthani?" (which means "My God, my God, why have you forsaken me?") (Matthew 27:45–46)**

Sin always causes a divide. Unfortunately, we do not really see this, as our selfishness and self-seeking nature is in full gear when we sin. We fail to see the impact of our actions. God had to look the other way when Jesus was on the cross because He was now carrying our sins. Can this be helpful for us when we are faced with temptation, knowing that we never want to be in a situation where God is forced to look away from us because of our sin? Separation causes grief, which means God is grieved by sin. Paul encouraged the Ephesian church to not grieve the Holy Spirit (Ephesians 4:30). When we remember the cross, let us remember the pain it caused and do our best to stay away from the source of that pain, which is sin.

There is a good way to look at separation however, as the cross is also the place where we were separated from our sins. This is where sin lost its power over us. This should also help us when we are tempted. Now that our sins have been taken away, we longer have to serve that sinful desire. We are no longer bound to operate under its influence; it is no longer a part of our identity.

2. THE CROSS IS A PLACE OF PROPITIATION.

> **My dear children, I write this to you so that you will not sin. But if anybody does sin, we have an advocate with the Father—Jesus Christ, the Righteous One. He is the atoning sacrifice for our sins, and not only for ours but also for the sins of the whole world. (1 John 2:1–2)**

When we succumb to sin and serve it again, we must also remember the cross as a place where God's anger has been appeased. We must never run away from God because of the fear of wrath and judgment; rather, we must run to God because of the opportunity that mercy has provided, an opportunity for us to find forgiveness for our sins. Because Jesus died on the cross for our sins, He is the perfect advocate and intercessor, standing between us and God, shielding us from His wrath, and securing mercy on our behalf.

This is very helpful to know and always remember. Don't be the person that just keeps running away because of the fear of retribution, to the point where you now sink deeper and deeper in your sin. I do not know if God gets angrier every day you stay away and sink deeper in your sin, but I do know that the moment you return and repent, mercy shows up, and the level of anger does not matter at that point. Jesus is constantly advocating and interceding for us.

3. THE CROSS IS A PLACE OF REDEMPTION.

Christ redeemed us from the curse of the law by becoming a curse for us, for it is written: "Cursed is everyone who is hung on a pole." (Galatians 3:13)

If you need to remind yourself that you have been saved, that your sins have been taken away, then the cross is the place to be. When those accusations come from the enemy, when the guilt and shame of sin come to weigh you down and discourage you in this Christian race, then look no further than to the cross, where the price for salvation has been paid. The cross is the constant reminder that we do not need to do anything more for salvation to be possible; we just need to accept what has been done and move on. We do not owe death anything anymore; we are free because we have been redeemed.

Redemption is a buying-back process. It helps me understand that I am God's creation. Sin took me away from Him, and then He worked out a plan and a way to get me back to my rightful place. There is great joy and comfort in this. The cross symbolizes this very truth: how precious we are in God's sight, and how much love He has for us that He is willing to sacrifice everything to get us back into His fold. He took us from darkness and put us back in His Kingdom, restoring us to our position with and in Christ. He restored our identity and empowered us to now live the life He wants us to live.

4. THE BLOOD CAN CLEANSE ANY AND ALL SIN.

> **He did not enter by means of the blood of goats and calves; but he entered the Most Holy Place once for all by his own blood, thus obtaining eternal redemption. (Hebrews 9:12)**

As it is God who is offended by sin, so He decides what appeases Him. This is something we cannot fully understand on this side of existence. It is life that restores life, and life is in the blood. Back in the Old Testament, when the children of Israel were on their way to the promised land, God would at various times command that everything be sprinkled with blood for it to be purified. When they sinned, He demanded a shedding of animal life, its blood serving as a symbol of appeasement and purification. The problem with this blood, however, was that it did not have a once-and-for-all power; it had to constantly be shed. In hindsight, this makes sense. How can the blood of a bull ransom the life of a man made in the image of God? For that quality of life to be redeemed, one would need blood that is of greater value and purity than its own. The blood of Jesus is qualified to redeem us, and that is exactly what He did. With His blood, He gave a once-and-for-all sacrifice, because it was of purer, better, and of greater value. Find courage in the Scripture passage below.

> **The blood of goats and bulls and the ashes of a heifer sprinkled on those who are ceremonially unclean sanctify**

them so that they are outwardly clean. How much more, then, will the blood of Christ, who through the eternal Spirit offered himself unblemished to God, cleanse our consciences from acts that lead to death, so that we may serve the living God! (Hebrews 9:13–14)

Why do I say all this? You need to understand that there is no sin in your life right now that the blood of Jesus cannot deliver you from. There is no sin that you have committed and that you are sitting on that the blood of Jesus cannot forgive if you run to the Father and ask for forgiveness. You don't need to try to figure out why and how. If Jesus has told us that His blood was poured out for the forgiveness of our sin, then we must believe it to be so.

››› THINK AND TALK ABOUT IT ‹‹‹

In what other ways is the cross and the blood of Jesus of significance and importance to you? How has it helped you to live as a child of God?

THIS IS WHAT WE MUST DO

If you declare with your mouth, "Jesus is Lord," and believe in your heart that God raised him from the dead, you will be saved. (Romans 10:9)

There is so much to learn, discover, and appreciate about God's salvation work. It is impossible to fit everything into this guide, and there is actually no reason to do that. The goal is not to replace the Bible; instead, my hope is that I have put enough here to awaken a desire and a longing in your heart that moves you closer to God, His Spirit, and His Word. It is in your daily walk with Him that you get the true understanding and revelation needed to live a fruitful and righteous life.

With all that we have said, let's talk now about what is expected of us in all this. What are we supposed to do with what God has offered? How do we receive this salvation offering and benefit from the righteousness that is now available in Christ? This is what we will be talking about before we wrap up this session. Please, do not confuse this information with salvation requirements. I see a lot of confusion, arguments, and sometimes a downright misleading agenda when it comes to salvation and righteousness. I am pretty sure you have heard some of these yourself. Some say that you don't have to do anything to be saved, which is a misleading statement. When you think about it, what does "do anything" mean? Does it mean no action on your part at all, or are they talking about specific actions? The moment "do anything" has to be further explained or clarified, then the entire statement is wrong and misleading. God has done His part, and now we must do ours. In the next session, we will talk in greater detail about what we must do after we have been saved; for now, we want to talk about what we must do to be saved. I have summed it up in three main points.

1. ACKNOWLEDGE

> **To the Jews who had believed him, Jesus said, "If you hold to my teaching, you are really my disciples. Then you will know the truth, and the truth will set you free." They answered him, "We are Abraham's descendants and have never been slaves of anyone. How can you say that we shall be set free?" Jesus replied, "Very truly I tell you, everyone who sins is a slave to sin. Now a slave has no permanent place in the family, but a son belongs to it forever. So if the Son sets you free, you will be free indeed." (John 8:31–36)**

I pulled this exchange from a larger conversation between Jesus and the children of Israel sometime after He had fed the five thousand. I would encourage you to read the entire discourse, starting from John 8:12. You can also go back and read from John 6 to capture the full context for this back-and-forth exchange between them.

It is clear that the children of Israel did not understand what Jesus was talking about. They thought He was talking about being enslaved and ruled over by other empires and kingdoms, but He was talking about slavery to sin. Even after He had clarified His statement in John 8:34, they still did not receive His words but continued arguing. How can salvation being made available benefit the one who is being offered salvation if he or she refuses to acknowledge the need for salvation?

Let me take you back to the illustration I made about the lifeguard. Imagine a lifeguard jumping into the pool to save someone, but the one in trouble starts to struggle and argue with the lifeguard, saying, "I'm good; I don't need help," even though it is clear and obvious that he or she is drowning. You cannot be saved if you do not acknowledge that you need salvation. If you keep telling yourself you're good and you do not need God or Jesus, then you cannot benefit from His gift of salvation. When you acknowledge you need salvation, it means you are acknowledging that you are a sinner and that you are a slave to your sinful ways. You are also acknowledging that if things stay the way they are, then you ultimately will end up in eternal destruction and darkness. It means you understand the weight and the pain of sin, and you desire freedom. It also means you now realize there is a better way to live, a better way that only God can make possible.

This is what we call the point of conviction, a point where we are now ready to give our lives back to God so He can resume His lordship and authority over us once again. Up until the point where a man or woman is convicted, they do not feel they are enslaved by sin because they do not believe they are living in sin. For them, it is simply living in freedom, deciding to live however they choose. They do not believe there is a standard or that God has a standard. But when conviction happens and the eyes and heart of a person are open, change becomes totally possible.

Earlier I had used the Scripture passage below to make the point that God decided how salvation would come. I want to use the same Scripture passage to drive home the point about acknowledgement. I hope it helps to bring a deeper understanding to it.

> **They traveled from Mount Hor along the route to the Red Sea, to go around Edom. But the people grew impatient on the way; they spoke against God and against Moses, and said, "Why have you brought us up out of Egypt to die in the wilderness? There is no bread! There is no**

> **water! And we detest this miserable food!"**
>
> **Then the LORD sent venomous snakes among them; they bit the people and many Israelites died. The people came to Moses and said, "We sinned when we spoke against the LORD and against you. Pray that the LORD will take the snakes away from us." So Moses prayed for the people.**
>
> **The LORD said to Moses, "Make a snake and put it up on a pole; anyone who is bitten can look at it and live." So Moses made a bronze snake and put it up on a pole. Then when anyone was bitten by a snake and looked at the bronze snake, they lived. (Numbers 21:4–9)**

After God had sent snakes into their midst as a result of their rebellion, the children of Israel asked God to take the snakes away. This at first seemed like a very reasonable request under the circumstances, but let's give it a deeper thought. Judging by their past behavior and reputation, the children of Israel wanted God to act as if there was no sin, sweep it under the rug, pretend like they did not just do what they did, and take the snakes away. It would be as if they did nothing wrong. Instead, God did something different, and I'll explain why. He told them that whoever got bitten by the snake should look at the snake on the pole, and they'd be healed. Not only was God letting them know He was the one to decide how salvation would be received, but He was also making them understand that without the acknowledgement of sin, salvation would not be made available. Anyone who looked at the snake was acknowledging that they had been bitten, and if they were bitten, it means that they had sinned, and they were acknowledging their sin. Notice God did not say anyone who looked at the snake would not be bitten; He said anyone who was bitten could look and then be healed. How can we receive forgiveness when we do not acknowledge we have done anything that needs forgiving? It is simply not possible.

2. RETURN

> **Therefore tell the people: This is what the LORD Almighty says: "Return to me," declares the LORD Almighty, "and I will return to you," says the LORD Almighty. (Zechariah 1:3, emphasis added)**

Now that you have acknowledged that life was heading in the wrong direction and that you are in need of God's salvation, the next plausible thing to do is to make a turn around and head toward the one who can save you from your dysfunction. This brings up a very important point, which is that at no point in time should you have a victim mentality or the impression that you are not responsible for how far away you have strayed from God; don't be deceived into thinking that there does not have to be a conscientious effort on your end to find your way back to God. When you hear the word *return*, it means you walked away from something, and now you are being asked to come back. You left home and made a mess of things, and now that your eyes are open, you need to come back home. You have to initiate the return process. Even if you are in one way or the other incapacitated, you cry out from where you are.

> **From that time on Jesus began to preach, "Repent, for the kingdom of heaven has come near." (Matthew 4:17)**

This was Jesus' opening message when He began preaching. This was Jesus, the Son of God, God Himself in flesh, saying this, and if He is saying this, it means this is absolutely necessary in order to receive the gift that He has made available. To *repent* means to make a turnaround, have a change of heart and attitude toward something, or to return to something. Yes, Jesus died for the sins of the whole world. However, that does not mean the whole world has been forgiven of its sins; it simply means forgiveness is available for the whole world if the world decides to take the right steps toward it.

What does it mean when we hear songs that say the love of God chases, it fights, it is reckless and does not give up, that nothing gets in the way of God's love when it comes looking for us? Well, if you translate that to mean that you're never too far gone to turn around, that the love of God will never walk away from you, that every moment and breath will always be an opportunity for you to reach out and hold that love again, then I would say you interpreted it rightly. But if you interpret this to mean that you can keep walking into darkness, keep rejecting God and pursuing self and ungodliness, that the love of God will somehow forcefully save you and that somehow God is just so starved for love to the point that He is willing to take whatever He can get from you, then I think you are in for a rude awakening at the end of your life if nothing changes. The love of God is reckless, but so is sin and death.

Balancing these parables below will help us put things in the proper perspective. Let's consider the parables of the lost sheep, the lost coin, and the prodigal son.

> **Then Jesus told them this parable: "Suppose one of you has a hundred sheep and loses one of them. Doesn't he leave the ninety-nine in the open country and go after the lost sheep until he finds it? And when he finds it, he joyfully puts it on his shoulders and goes home. Then he**

calls his friends and neighbors together and says, 'Rejoice with me; I have found my lost sheep.' I tell you that in the same way there will be more rejoicing in heaven over one sinner who repents than over ninety-nine righteous persons who do not need to repent.

"Or suppose a woman has ten silver coins and loses one. Doesn't she light a lamp, sweep the house and search carefully until she finds it? And when she finds it, she calls her friends and neighbors together and says, 'Rejoice with me; I have found my lost coin.' In the same way, I tell you, there is rejoicing in the presence of the angels of God over one sinner who repents."

Jesus continued: "There was a man who had two sons. The younger one said to his father, 'Father, give me my share of the estate.' So he divided his property between them.

"Not long after that, the younger son got together all he had, set off for a distant country and there squandered his wealth in wild living. After he had spent everything, there was a severe famine in that whole country, and he began to be in need. So he went and hired himself out to a citizen of that country, who sent him to his fields to feed pigs. He longed to fill his stomach with the pods that the pigs were eating, but no one gave him anything.

"When he came to his senses, he said, 'How many of my father's hired servants have food to spare, and here I am starving to death! I will set out and go back to my father and say to him: Father, I have sinned against heaven and against you. I am no longer worthy to be called your son; make me like one of your hired servants.' So he got up and went to his father.

"But while he was still a long way off, his father saw him and was filled with compassion for him; he ran to his son, threw his arms around him and kissed him.

"The son said to him, 'Father, I have sinned against heaven and against you. I am no longer worthy to be called your son.'

"But the father said to his servants, 'Quick! Bring the best robe and put it on him. Put a ring on his finger and sandals on his feet. Bring the fattened calf and kill it. Let's have a feast and celebrate. For this son of mine was dead and is alive again; he was lost and is found.' So they began to celebrate." (Luke 15:3–24)

Let's begin with these points:

1. All three parables speak about the same thing.
2. All three parables speak about sin, repentance, and salvation.
3. All three parables must be interpreted considering sin, repentance, and salvation, and not one or the other.
4. All three parables describe a moment of rejoicing and celebration at the end.

In the first parable, we are told someone has a hundred sheep and loses one; he goes after the sheep, finds it, and brings it back home. How can we interpret this parable, considering sin, repentance, and salvation? Hopefully, you do not interpret the loss of the sheep as God losing us. God does not lose anyone or lead anyone into sin; rather, we are the ones that stray away from the fold. The sheep in the parable wandered away.

You and I are the sheep. Our self-led and selfish desires lead us away from God's will and into sin, and then we get lost. The sheep owner goes out looking for the sheep. This is indicative of God in His mercy reaching out to us, offering us a way back to right standing, back to holiness, back to purity and love. The owner finds the sheep and bring it back home, rejoicing. The right interpretation is also key here. Did the owner find the sheep and bring it back home regardless of whether the sheep wanted to come home or not? Was the sheep forced, did it fight back, or resist being brought back? The only way to interpret this rightly is to get to the end of the parable where it says that there is joy in heaven when a sinner repents. This sheep was not forced back home; although the owner came looking for it, the sheep also realized it had gone astray and repented. Repentance brings us back home.

To understand the use of the word *sheep* in this parable, we have to recognize that it is more figurative than literal. It speaks to the comparability of the character of the sheep to human nature, especially our vulnerability and susceptibility to stray and wander off.

In the second parable, a coin is lost. Same as in the first parable, God did not lose us; we did not fall out of His pocket or something (well, maybe we jumped out). You should not look at the coin in a literal sense, the same way we did not look at the sheep in a literal sense. Instead, think of the value of a coin. We walk away from God when we ignore or take for granted the esteemed position we have in Him; we devalue ourselves and walk into sin and chaos. As with the first parable, God's love will always come looking for us, because He is just that faithful. There is never a time in your life when you are away from Him that you are not constantly reminded that there is grace and opportunity for you to come back home. The devil may tell you otherwise, sin may make you feel otherwise, but you'd best believe there is not a day in your life that the goodness and mercy of God is absent. Every day He gives you the opportunity for repentance. When we recognize how far we have fallen, we repent and accept this value back. Once again, do not interpret the woman finding the coin to mean that there is no responsibility on the part of the sinner to make his or her way back home. As with the first parable, when you get to the end it says that there is rejoicing when a sinner repents.

I believe the third parable really knocks it out of the park, and this is why it is best to approach the Word of God with a focus on contextual completeness. Jesus spoke these three parables in succession. Although there is nothing wrong with reading only one of them, when you do, you may not get the full context of what Jesus was communicating. In this parable, we have a son who decided to wander off because he felt there was a better life and a better place for him outside of his father's house. He was simply foolish and lacked the understanding of how good he really had it. This ought to remind you of the sheep and the coin.

Here is where this parable now goes in a different direction from the previous two. The father of this prodigal son never leaves home to go find the boy, unlike the sheep owner who went looking for the sheep and the woman who started searching everywhere for her lost coin. Interesting, right? But even though he did not physically leave the house, his love accompanied this boy. We know this by the boy's conversation with himself in Luke 15:17. When the memories of how life was in his father's house started flooding his mind, he realized there was nothing but love, life, and goodness at home. What the first two parables are teaching when the sheep and coin owner go out in search is the same thing the boy's remembrance of life in his father's house is communicating. This is the love and mercy of God in action; it is always with us, not only to convict us of our sin but also to remind us of the life we have forsaken and left behind. It reminds us that our space still awaits us, and God is ever willing to take us back. The boy realizes the error of his way, repents, and returns home, and like in the other two parables, there is a celebration.

Salvation cannot happen without repentance. Nobody is going to be coerced into salvation, forced, deceived, or manipulated. God is not going to do it for us either. No, repentance is the sinner's responsibility, and salvation is God's.

3. CONFESS

If you declare with your mouth, "Jesus is Lord," and believe in your heart that God raised him from the dead, you will be saved. (Romans 10:9)

After the conviction and the turnaround, this is where we formally, verbally, and wholly accept everything that salvation represents and offers. We are before God, vulnerable, open, repentant and sincere, ready for change, ready for a new life. We submit and surrender to His lordship and authority. You see, our life of sin was making a statement that Jesus Christ was not Lord over our lives and that we were in full control. When we repent, we need to renounce the throne and hand it back to Him, because He is indeed the Lord over our soul. Through our confession, we lay down our life of sin, by believing that His journey to the grave and back was to free us from the burden of sin. Thus, when we believe that God raised Jesus from the dead, it means that we believe that He has the power to free us from the slavery of sin. Because of that, we lay down our life of sin in order to take up the new life His resurrection from the dead offers.

There is no need to be ashamed before God. We must be bold to speak at this point. He did not invite us into His presence to condemn us; rather, we were brought in to be changed, redeemed, sanctified, and purified. We must let our hearts, and our mouths declare the truth about His love and salvation. He is Lord, and He came to save us. He has the power to save us, and He will.

››› PRAYER OPPORTUNITIES AND FOCUS ‹‹‹

- *This session presents an opportunity for anyone who's reading this but has not fully committed his or her life to Christ. Will you in this moment cross this bridge once and for all? I believe if you go to God in prayer and let Him into your heart, He can help remove whatever obstacles are preventing you from surrendering completely to Him.*
- *Some may also be struggling with believing that a new life awaits on the other side of their confession. If you are in that category, will you let the Spirit of God open your eyes and heart to what He has already proclaimed in His Word—that new life is available for those who believe? Are you willing to take that doubt before God and spend some time praying about it?*
- *Are you in the category of folks who believe there is no need to change course, and that life is secure even when lived in dysfunction? Will you let this session move you toward conviction? Are you willing to call on God to help you understand more, to give you a better understanding of what His love and salvation truly mean?*

SESSION 3

NOW THAT WE ARE HERE

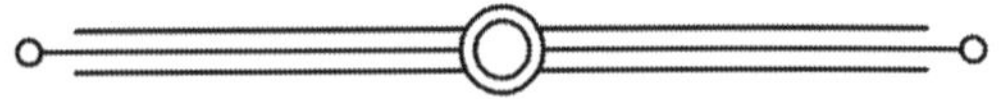

For you were once darkness, but now you are light in the Lord. Live as children of light (for the fruit of the light consists in all goodness, righteousness and truth) and find out what pleases the Lord. Have nothing to do with the fruitless deeds of darkness, but rather expose them.

(Ephesians 5:8–11)

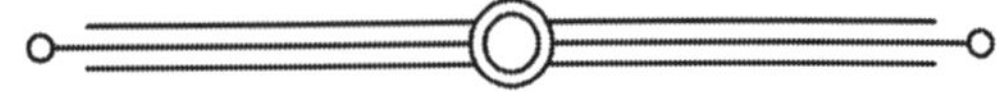

INTRODUCTION

Now that we have been saved, what is expected of us in this new state that we are in? In this session, we are going to take a closer look at what the Christian life is really supposed to be. If we believe God did not save us just for the sake of saving, then we ought to understand that things will be different in this new life. I think one of the most misunderstood concepts in our time and present culture is freedom and what exactly it means for a born-again child of God. The majority of the erroneous and misleading theological concepts in the Christian faith is found in this category—the process of figuring out what comes next after we receive salvation from God. My prayer is that God will lead us through all we will be discussing and will help us arrive at the truth—His truth.

ICEBREAKER

Have you experienced relocation, a change of environment, a new job, or even a new relationship? What was your mindset going into these new spaces? Were you expecting things to be the same, or did you anticipate there would be a need to adjust to the new? What were the challenges, if any?

EVERYTHING NEW

Praise be to the God and Father of our Lord Jesus Christ! In his great mercy he has given us new birth into a living hope through the resurrection of Jesus Christ from the dead. (1 Peter 1:3)

Let us start off by stating the obvious: anyone who gives his or her life to Christ did so with the expectation that the way life would be, going forward, would be different from what it was. Here we are talking primarily about our spiritual life, the life that really matters, the life that will endure this present existence and transition over to the next. We believe that surrendering to Christ ushers in a new existence. We are called a new creation: the old things are done with, and new things are ushered in. In this next section, we will explore what this newness is and how we should view it. This newness is and should be every believer's testimony: they will be able to say categorically and definitively that before Christ, life was this way, and now with Christ, life is another way. Even in the ups and downs and challenges of life, this testimony must never change. There is a difference between when Christ is in a situation and when He is not.

Let me present this newness in three distinct and successive layers. By *successive*, I mean you cannot jump the first one and experience the second or jump the second to experience the third. You also cannot experience the first and ignore the second and third. To experience the newness of life that Christ offers, you must go through these three levels in order.

1. NEWNESS IN IDENTITY

Therefore, if anyone is in Christ, the new creation has come: The old has gone, the new is here! (2 Corinthians 5:17)

I am not sure how it is in other parts of the world; it may be similar or not. However, if you are living in the United States, the word *identity* should not be strange to you. I dare say it may be the most fascinating thing in our society now. In our society, it is all about identity and people identifying with whatever it is they want to identify with. At some point, we will run out of things to identify with. For our purposes, I would like to focus on an identity that really matters, one that comes with eternal implications and consequences.

When we give our lives to Christ, we are moved from one household to another. It is amazing that even though we are all God's creation, we are not all God's children in the real sense. Our sin moved us away from our status as children of God. Our lifestyle made a statement, and that statement was that we were not under God's control, and we wanted to do our own thing. We refused to identify with anything that was remotely righteous or godly. Our ideology did not come from God but from the world and ourselves. No one could look at us and see Christ in us. His image and likeness that we were supposed to reflect based on His original purpose and intent for us was just not there. At that point, we were simply God's creation and not His children. However, that all changes the moment we decide to turn around, repent, and be reconciled. Our identity has now changed from being just a creation to children. We now identify with God, and we should be identified by God and nothing else. This is the new creation that Paul referred to in the Scripture verse above; this is a life reset and restart. The Scripture verse below also talks about a change of location, a change of address: we have been relocated to a new place, a new space.

For he has rescued us from the dominion of darkness and brought us into the kingdom of the Son he loves. (Colossians 1:13)

The most important thing we should take away from this point about identity is that when we are in Christ, we are seen differently. God sees us differently, the devil sees us differently, and the world should also see us differently. Unfortunately, this also applies when we decide to live outside of Christ; we are seen and perceived differently. It is all about identity. Even as everyone around us is identifying with their various identities, we as children of God must make sure that our new identity is first and foremost made clear to the world through our confession. We must make our own choice to be saved and embrace the new tag that has been placed on us.

The last (and probably the most important) thing to say about identity is that it ultimately forms the life of the one who identifies. He or she no longer needs to proclaim their identity; by the way they live, they reveal their identity.

››› THINK AND TALK ABOUT IT ‹‹‹

As simple as this may sound, how do you see yourself, especially as a child of God?

2. NEWNESS IN THINKING

> **Do not conform to the pattern of this world, but be transformed by the renewing of your mind. Then you will be able to test and approve what God's will is—his good, pleasing and perfect will. (Romans 12:2)**

Quite a few people see being born again and following Christ as being brainwashed. They seem to have a thing against people following rules and regulations and adhering to a type or mode of thinking and living. This is a ridiculous stance because there is no way of life that you decide to follow that does not require you to think a certain way or have a particular mindset. The problem they have is that they are not in control of what God's way of thinking is, and they want to live life on their own terms. No one acts without thinking; even when you ask someone, "What were you thinking?" and they respond, "I was not thinking," that is not a true statement. No action is carried out, especially sinful action, without thought. Just because someone exercised poor judgment does not mean there was an absence of thought and analysis before their action; it just happened to be that the thought and analysis led them down a wrong path. There is a reason why the Scripture verse below talks about thoughts and ways together, because they go hand in hand; one gives birth to the other.

> **"For my thoughts are not your thoughts, neither are your ways my ways," declares the Lord. (Isaiah 55:8)**

Are Christians being brainwashed? No, but we are being mind-washed. If that affects how the brain works for the better and for God's glory, then so be it. To experience life in a new way, a new way of mind and thinking is needed; new house, new rules. God has His way of doing things, and the world has its way. If you want to be in God's house, then you must do things His way. This means you must change your perception and perspective and make sure it aligns with how He wants things done. Your thought process now needs to change, and especially your conclusions about life matters. You cannot think God's way and then arrive at a worldly conclusion.

Let us look at a few Scriptures passages to drive this point home.

> **What shall we say, then? Shall we go on sinning so that grace may increase? By no means! We are those who have died to sin; how can we live in it any longer? Or don't you know that all of us who were baptized into Christ Jesus were baptized into his death? (Romans 6:1–3)**

> **What then? Shall we sin because we are not under the law but under grace? By no means! Don't you know that when you offer yourselves to someone as obedient slaves, you are slaves of the one you obey—whether you are slaves to sin, which leads to death, or to obedience, which leads to righteousness? (Romans 6:15–16)**

These are excerpts from Romans chapter 6. In verses 3 and 16, Paul asks a question, and that question is, "Don't you know?" Know what exactly? Well, Paul, the writer, is asking if we have gained the knowledge that things are different on the side that we are now on. Paul is saying that it is time to start thinking differently. Previously we were alive in sin, so our thought process was different, but now we are dead to sin, and things ought to be different.

> **Do you not know, brothers and sisters—for I am speaking to those who know the law—that the law has authority over someone only as long as that person lives? For example, by law a married woman is bound to her husband as long as he is alive, but if her husband dies, she is released from the law that binds her to him. So then, if she has sexual relations with another man while her husband is still alive, she is called an adulteress. But if her husband dies, she is released from that law and is not an adulteress if she marries another man.**
>
> **So, my brothers and sisters, you also died to the law through the body of Christ, that you might belong to another, to him who was raised from the dead, in order that we might bear fruit for God. For when we were in the realm of the flesh, the sinful passions aroused by the law were at work in us, so that we bore fruit for death. But now, by dying to what once bound us, we have been released from the law so that we serve in the new way of the Spirit, and not in the old way of the written code. (Romans 7:1–6)**

Romans 7 starts with the same question, "Do you not know?" Paul then goes on to use marriage and the death of a spouse to illustrate what our relationship to sin was and what it should now be. He says all this to illustrate how we need to start seeing things differently. It is impossible to live a fulfilling Christian and godly life without a change in mindset and perspective. Now that we have a different source of fuel flowing through our being, we cannot have the same mentality and thinking as when we were not in Christ. This next Scripture verse says it all, and we will end this point with it.

> **Those who live according to the flesh have their minds set on what the flesh desires; but those who live in accordance with the Spirit have their minds set on what the Spirit desires. The mind governed by the flesh is death, but the mind governed by the Spirit is life and peace. The mind governed by the flesh is hostile to God; it does not submit to God's law, nor can it do so. (Romans 8:5–7)**

››› THINK AND TALK ABOUT IT ‹‹‹

Since you gave your life to Christ, how has the journey of the mindset change been?

3. NEWNESS IN LIVING

> **So I tell you this, and insist on it in the Lord, that you must no longer live as the Gentiles do, in the futility of their thinking. (Ephesians 4:17)**

I hope by now you see why I said that these three layers are built on one another, starting from the first. You first must identify with Christ, and then the way you see things starts to change, and ultimately the way you do things will change. I think it makes perfect sense; don't you? We will be expanding this point in the next section of this session, but I felt the need to introduce it here in order to complete the newness levels.

The ultimate question that needs to be tackled is this: How do we know we are saved if nothing in life changes? Put another way, what is the evidence of our salvation, the evidence of our claim to being changed? If we claim that the old has gone and the new is here, it would be reasonable to expect that the newness would be obvious in our character and behavior, especially now that we are living life under a new set of rules and authority. I call this behavioral modification, and even that may be seen as controversial, as some erroneously believe that our salvation has nothing to do with what we do. I would say it really depends on the side of the coin that you are looking at. Yes, Jesus paid for our salvation, but He did not hang on that cross, shed His blood, and give up His life so that our life would remain the same. We have established that He came because of sin, so if He conquered sin by His death and gave us power by His resurrection, what is the reasonable expectation here?

››› THINK AND TALK ABOUT IT ‹‹‹

If you have yet to give your life to Christ, is the expectation of the new life a hindrance, or is it simply a misunderstanding of this new life? If you have given your life to Christ, do you have the right expectation as to how your life ought to be moving forward?

CONTRAST

You are all children of the light and children of the day. We do not belong to the night or to the darkness. (1 Thessalonians 5:5)

Is the message and the Gospel of grace misleading, or are we the ones who do not understand? Do we deliberately misinterpret it in order to fit some narrative or form a justification for the way we choose to live? That we are saved by grace and not by works seems to mean that there is no responsibility on our part to adhere to any rules for godly living, forgetting that the one who saved us is the same one who laid out the rules. Did God save us from Himself? Did He lay down unrealistic rules but then have a change of mind? Why is it that the moment we start to talk about righteous and holy living, we get into this theological and societal contention about what it really means to be saved, even entertaining the idea that salvation can somehow be experienced void of accountability and effort on the part of the one being saved?

A while ago, I was listening to an episode of *The Breakfast Club*, an American syndicated radio show hosted by Charlamagne tha God. On this particular episode,[1] there was another celebrity guest: Trevor Noah, who at that time was the host of the *Daily Show*, an award-winning nighttime TV program. At some point, they started discussing religion, contrasting the Jehovah's Witnesses faith with what Trevor referred to as "the fun religion." He was alluding to the expressive side of the evangelical Christian faith: the singing, dancing, rejoicing, the hope of the good news, and the absence of human legalistic and always erroneous stipulations on how

---

1 To watch the clip, see Molifi Kalane, "Trevor Noah's Take of Christianity and the Bible," YouTube video, January 14, 2020, https://www.youtube.com/watch?v=XrfIHpXtnNs.

to connect to God and get to heaven. He was in no way mocking the Christian faith. But then he made a statement that I thought was very interesting, to the effect that all you had to do to get into heaven was to accept Jesus as your Lord and Savior. Now, if we leave this statement in the context of the show and the discussion that was being had, I will say that I agree. First of all, it would be unrealistic to expect or even demand an expert analysis or exegesis of doctrine on the show, as they were not giving a sermon or leading Bible study. Second, and most especially, it is a true and factual statement: access to eternal life and the salvation through which it comes is received by accepting Jesus Christ as Lord and Savior; nothing more, and nothing less.

However, the validation of a truth is reflected not only in its proclamation but also in the interpretation and ultimate application of that truth to daily living. You see, truth and revelation are never given in a vacuum. The goal is to affect life and behavior, so this statement, as factual as it is, can be very misleading if the phrase "all you had to do was accept" is interpreted in a way that leads to a wrong application of the truth. The question is, how do we know the right application of the truth? Well, we simply take this truth out of the context of the discussion on *The Breakfast Club* and stick it back into the context of its source, and that source is the Word of God. Trevor Noah did not make up the truth in that statement; it was simply his translation of this all-popular Scripture verse:

For God so loved the world that he gave his one and only Son, that whoever believes in him shall not perish but have eternal life. (John 3:16)

This Scripture verse faces the same challenge that Trevor's statement faces. In this case, the interpretation of "believes in him" becomes problematic if it is not interpreted considering everything else in the Word of God. The question is, should there be a change in the life and behavior of a believer based on his or her belief, and should there be a contrast between the life he or she had before belief or acceptance and his or her life after? Did Jesus come, die, and resurrect to change our behavior, or is there an expectation and acceptance of the status quo? These are the realities we must face in our Christian journey and faith. I believe the Word of God has enough truth to steer us in the right direction, assuming we are willing to go in that direction. Each one of us must start to constantly ask the question, "Why was I saved, and for what purpose?" Let us look at some Scripture passages!

> **Follow God's example, therefore, as dearly loved children and walk in the way of love, just as Christ loved us and gave himself up for us as a fragrant offering and sacrifice to God.**
>
> **But among you there must not be even a hint of sexual immorality, or of any kind of impurity, or of greed, because these are improper for God's holy people.**
>
> **Nor should there be obscenity, foolish talk or coarse joking, which are out of place, but rather thanksgiving. For of this you can be sure:**
>
> **No immoral, impure or greedy person—such a person is an idolater—has any inheritance in the kingdom of Christ and of God.**
>
> **Let no one deceive you with empty words, for because of such things God's wrath comes on those who are disobedient.**

Therefore do not be partners with them.
(Ephesians 5:1–7)

Take a few moments to meditate on this Scripture passage, and then ask yourself why verse 3 starts with the word *But*. In the English language, we use the word *but* to introduce something that was not earlier talked or thought about and most especially something different from what's just been said. We use it to clear any misconceptions or misunderstanding of what may have been presented before. To understand all of what's being said in this Scripture passage, I would encourage you to open your Bible and read from Ephesians 4:17, as this is where Paul starts his description of and instructions on godly living, drawing a contrast between God's new way and the world's old way. So, is his use of the word *but* nullifying all the instructions from Ephesians 4 up to that point? Absolutely not! If you read the very first two verses of chapter 5, it will become clear what Paul is trying to say. It is simply this: Walk in the way of love, but that love can never be reflected by the behaviors that follow, or be interpreted to mean there is no need to be holy. Embrace the love of God, but do not abuse or misconstrue it, because salvation is a call to be holy and not an exemption from it.

As an example, Paul warned against sexual immorality. He is essentially saying there is a contrast between God and the world when it comes to sex. For the world, sex can happen between two (and I dare say more) people who mutually consent to the act. Contrast that with God's requirement on sex: it can only happen between a man (God-created) and a woman (God-created) who are in a marital commitment. Do you see the contrast? Mutual consent against marital commitment. You can do the same analysis with everything else that Paul has called out as behavior that is not indicative of the new life. There is an expectation for us to be different. Even when we stumble and fall into any of these sins, it does not change what is expected of us, and we must never forget that.

> **You were taught, with regard to your former way of life, to put off your old self, which is being corrupted by its deceitful desires; to be made new in the attitude of your minds; and to put on the new self, created to be like God in true righteousness and holiness. (Ephesians 4:22–24)**

We see contrast here again: old self versus new self. Who is the old self? The one who was outside of God's authority, who did things their own way and determined their own path, who was self-centered, self-focused, sinful, and conceited. Who is the new self? The one that has now submitted and surrendered to God's authority, the one who now uses the Word of God as a guide to living, who no longer takes perspective from the world.

We are instructed to put something off and put on something else, but does this mean that we have the power in ourselves to live this new life and follow the new path? We will answer that question in the next section!

››› THINK AND TALK ABOUT IT ‹‹‹

How do you measure your growth as a born-again child of God? If you do not evaluate or assess yourself, is there any reason behind that?

WHERE IS THE POWERHOUSE?

> **For what the law was powerless to do because it was weakened by the flesh, God did by sending his own Son in the likeness of sinful flesh to be a sin offering. And so he condemned sin in the flesh, in order that the righteous requirement of the law might be fully met in us, who do not live according to the flesh but according to the Spirit. (Romans 8:3–4)**

Let's discuss the role that the Spirit of God plays in our transformation journey, so that we do not get the wrong impression about how life after salvation is supposed to be. Just as we cannot earn salvation outside of faith in Jesus Christ, so also we cannot fulfill the expectations of salvation without help. Everything God needs from us needs a God-type of strength. So, God being fully aware of the damage that sin and disobedience has done to our flesh, has made provision for grace to be available for anyone and everyone who has decided to surrender their lives to Christ.

> **For the grace of God has appeared that offers salvation to all people. It teaches us to say "No" to ungodliness and worldly passions, and to live self-controlled, upright and godly lives in this present age, while we wait for the blessed hope—the appearing of the glory of our great God and Savior, Jesus Christ, who gave himself for us to redeem us from all wickedness and to purify for himself a people that are his very own, eager to do what is good. (Titus 2:11–14)**

Grace means different things to different people, but grace in this context is the help we get from God to live godly lives. It comes in the form of power, counsel, encouragement, warnings, and even sometimes rebuke with the purpose of realignment. Some may think that a rebuke is not an act of grace but think about it this way: God could react to our sins in more judgmental and rash ways, but He chooses to bring the sin to our attention and then offer forgiveness. That is a wonderful thing!

Salvation does not make us self-sufficient beings, possessing this great power to take on the world and the devil by ourselves (even though there is false teaching and theology being taught about this). The goal is not for the one who is now born again to go figure out by themselves how to stop lying, stealing, killing, committing adultery and fornication; rather, it is to let the Holy Spirit now be the guide and navigator through all the challenges the believer is about to face. You will fast find out that the temptations, the natural and sinful urges that you had before you were saved, still lurk around and present themselves after you're saved. It will be a constant and daily battle to keep standing until your life on this side is over. If you erroneously subscribe to the falsehood that you are now somehow Jesus Christ 2.0 and start to play around, the devil will get you—and get you good. Please don't get it wrong: being born again doesn't make you into a deity—far from it!

Before salvation, surrendering to sinful desires and gratifying the flesh would not be foreign to us, as this is what is expected. The only power available to us then was the power to live in sin. The body has plenty of that fuel to keep living in dysfunction, and the knowledge base of our existence at that time was the lies we had been told. We lived however we liked, did whatever we liked, and made sinful and selfish satisfaction our first and foremost priority. However, the moment we switched sides, we had a need for the power that overrides what the flesh wants and desires. Now we need a different kind of fuel, fuel that will empower godly living and choices, fuel that drives us in a different direction, and fuel that sustains us where God requires us to be. Read the words of Jesus below.

> **And I will ask the Father, and he will give you another advocate to help you and be with you forever—the Spirit of truth. The world cannot accept him, because it neither sees him nor knows him. But you know him, for he lives with you and will be in you. (John 14:16–17)**

I find it very intriguing that Jesus introduces the Holy Spirit as another advocate. What is an advocate? According to Webster, an advocate is someone who defends or maintains a cause or proposal, someone who supports or promotes the interest of a cause or a group. The work of salvation that Jesus did for us was advocacy work before God the Father. He presented Himself as a sacrifice to promote our cause, the cause to be given another chance at life and the opportunity to be reconciled back to the Father. The Holy Spirit is another advocate who works on our behalf and promotes our lives before the Father, to ensure that the work of salvation done on our behalf is not a waste and that we receive the full benefits of it.

> **And you also were included in Christ when you heard the message of truth, the gospel of your salvation. When you believed, you were marked in him with a seal, the promised Holy Spirit, who is a deposit guaranteeing our inheritance until the redemption of those who are God's possession—to the praise of his glory. (Ephesians 1:13–14)**

The Spirit of God was given to us to guarantee our inheritance. When you combine this with the words of Jesus, you'll get a better understanding of the role the Spirit of God plays in our Christian journey. God has a lot to give us, including a world and a life that we currently cannot comprehend. As a sign of good faith and as an acknowledgement of what He knows we need, He gives us His Spirit. How else can we ensure that the salvation we have received materializes into this wonderful inheritance? Well, we align ourselves with the one who not only knows what that inheritance is but who can also represent us before the one who has promised that inheritance. As Jesus represents us before the Father, so He also sends the Holy Spirit to work within us to make sure that we are living according to His purpose and pattern, especially in a way that will make inheritance possible at the end of our lives. For all those things that are impossible for us to do because of the sinful nature we carry, the Holy Spirit gives us His strength to make those things possible. All those things we never knew to do, He opens our eyes to see those things. He is not only the sign from God that He has something in store for us, but He is also the one that is tasked with the responsibility of making sure we stay on track. The Spirit of God does a lot for us, but for the sake of simplicity, let us bucket them in these three points.

1. REVELATION AND GUIDANCE

I have much more to say to you, more than you can now bear. But when he, the Spirit of truth, comes, he will guide you into all the truth. He will not speak on his own; he will speak only what he hears, and he will tell you what is yet to come. He will glorify me because it is

from me that he will receive what he will make known to you. All that belongs to the Father is mine. That is why I said the Spirit will receive from me what he will make known to you. (John 16:12–15)

Here we can see a type of hand-off going on. At this point, Jesus was preparing His disciples for His physical departure, and He was communicating to them what life would be like after that departure. You see, from the time that they left everything to follow Jesus, His disciples had become totally dependent on Him. Everything they needed to know or to do, where to go, how to live and act and relate—it all came from Jesus. They practically lived wherever He lived. So, what would happen when He was no longer with them? Were they supposed to try to figure things out themselves, return to the way things were, try to remember as best as they could all He had told and taught them? What was that going to look like exactly? Put yourself in their shoes and just think about what you would need. Constant reminders, someone to let you know what is true and not true, someone to help you navigate and walk the way Jesus would have walked. All of these are found in the Holy Spirit. He is the third and in no way the least Person in the Trinity. He is the carrier, the incubator, and the custodian of God's will and power, and He is the one that is now left behind to continue where the Father and the Son left off.

The believer needs guidance, especially now that he or she is living life under a new creed. There will be countless and constant moments of ignorance that require revelation for him or her to live and move in the right direction. Jesus lets us know that the Spirit of God is available to provide that revelation. Although the believer has the written Word of God, it takes the help of the Holy Spirit to understand what is being read and then apply it to life.

For who knows a person's thoughts except their own spirit within them? In the same way no one knows the thoughts of God except the Spirit of God. (1 Corinthians 2:11)

Everything that Jesus would have told us if He were here, the Spirit of God is more than capable to do the same. He knows what is in the mind of Christ; after all, He is described above as the custodian of all that Jesus thinks about and plans for. If we form a relationship with the Holy Spirit, it will be as if Jesus were physically with us, because we will know His plans for our lives and never have to be confused or wander aimlessly in life. Ever heard the phrase, "Where there is a will, there is a way"? Let me use this phrase in a different way than you are familiar with. Think of a will in the sense of a legal declaration of a person's wishes regarding the disposal of his or her property or estate after death (as according to Webster). If a will is available upon death, there should not be any confusion as to what needs to be done with the property or estate, unless parties are not aware that a will was left behind. Thus, if God has a plan for us, which is His will and purpose for our lives, and we have someone to make us aware of that, then there should be no reason why a believer should be confused or ignorant for too long on this journey. Just as Jesus said, the Spirit of God will make us aware of God's plan for us, thereby showing us the way.

››› THINK AND TALK ABOUT IT ‹‹‹

Are you making it a habit to ask the Holy Spirit for guidance? Do you ask Him for wisdom or revelation every time you open

the Bible, or do you try to make sense of things yourself? Do you have experiences that highlight your growth in this area of dependence?

2. POWER OVER SIN

> **But if Christ is in you, then even though your body is subject to death because of sin, the Spirit gives life because of righteousness. And if the Spirit of him who raised Jesus from the dead is living in you, he who raised Christ from the dead will also give life to your mortal bodies because of his Spirit who lives in you. Therefore, brothers and sisters, we have an obligation—but it is not to the flesh, to live according to it. For if you live according to the flesh, you will die; but if by the Spirit you put to death the misdeeds of the body, you will live. (Romans 8:10–14)**

Let me try to present this Scripture passage as simply as I possibly can so that we can understand the role of the Spirit of God when it comes to power over sin. Now that Jesus Christ has paid the price for our sin—and remember, that price is death, "for the wages of sin is death" (Romans 6:23)—you would think that there ought to be no more recourse for sin. In this case, that would mean sin has no legal or enforceable right to come to us to collect any longer. Jesus paid the price; it is settled and that is it, so sin, you need to walk away and move on. Well, unless you were taken straight to heaven the moment you gave your life to Christ, it ends up not being this simple, especially as we now have to go back into the sinful and dysfunctional world and society where we fell into all the craziness in the first place. Also, sin is still very much present in our lives, and its goal is to take as many as possible to the grave by peddling the same lies just so we sign our lives away again and become enslaved all over again. Above all, and most importantly, the fact that Jesus had to pay the price that set us free meant that we had no power whatsoever to fight off sin; if we could, it would not have enslaved us in the first place. So what do we do? To keep sin at bay, the body must stay dead, but since we need to live in the same body because we still have a job to do on earth, how do we live?

This is where the Spirit of God comes in. He comes to provide a different fuel for this body to use to live. Even though sin will still try to get in and take control, if the body is connected to the fuel of the Holy Spirit, it is able to resist sin and prevent it from causing further damage. If you look above at the Scripture passage that says the Spirit of God gives life to our mortal bodies (Romans 8:11), this will make sense. "Mortal body" simply means that this same body that sin ravaged and that had to die because of that, this body is the same body into which the Holy Spirit will put new life for it to now live in righteousness and holiness. This should also help us understand the part that says that even though the body is subject to death because of sin, the Spirit gives it life because of righteousness. In essence, even though Scripture says whoever is in Christ is a new creature, we still must deal with the mortal body until it is exchanged for our resurrected body. If that is the case, we need something outside of ourselves to overcome sin in our lives, and that something is none other than the power of the Holy Spirit. Let us look at another Scripture passage.

> **Therefore, there is now no condemnation for those who are in Christ Jesus, because through Christ Jesus the law of the Spirit who gives life has set you free from the law of sin and death. For what the law was powerless to do because it was weakened by the flesh, God did by sending his own Son in the likeness of sinful flesh to be a sin offering. And so he condemned sin in the flesh, in order that the righteous requirement of the law might be fully met in us, who do not live according to the flesh but according to the Spirit. (Romans 8:1–4)**

There is a lot to unpack in this passage, but my focus is on the end of verse 4, where Paul talks about those who do not live according to the flesh but according to the Spirit. First, what does "live according to the Spirit" mean? I think it is exactly as we talked about while studying the earlier Scripture passage. It means using the power the Holy Spirit provides to live. It means living based on His strength and guidance. Therefore, if we live by the Spirit, we reap the benefit of what Jesus worked for us on the cross (the condemnation of sin in our flesh, which stripped sin of power), and we can fulfill the demands that righteousness has placed on us. God does not demand anything from us for which He does not give to us the grace and power to meet that demand. We may focus on God's requirement in isolation and form the idea that we are supposed to live righteously by our own strength, but that is not the case. Until we lay this body down and depart this world, we will need to partner and walk with the Holy Spirit every step of the way and be totally dependent and reliant on Him, because we simply cannot contend with sin by ourselves.

››› THINK AND TALK ABOUT IT ‹‹‹

Do you ever think you have to contend with or are contending with sin on your own? Do you know how to receive strength from the Spirit of God for you to live righteously?

3. INTERCESSION

> **In the same way, the Spirit helps us in our weakness. We do not know what we ought to pray for, but the Spirit himself intercedes for us through wordless groans. And he who searches our hearts knows the mind of the Spirit, because the Spirit intercedes for God's people in accordance with the will of God. (Romans 8:26–27)**

What is *intercession*? Webster defines it as a prayer, petition, or entreaty in favor of another. To *intercede* is defined by Webster as intervening between two parties with a view to reconciling differences. This is as simple as it will get. We have God on one side, and we are on the other side, and between us is the Spirit of God, working on bringing both sides together in unity and oneness. The Spirit of God takes the plan and purpose of God, brings it over to us, and helps us walk in the light of it. As He is helping us to realize and live in our newfound reality, so He is assuring God that all is going to be well with us. He ensures that mercy is constantly flowing from the throne of grace. He comes to our side and helps us in areas of weakness. He even coaches us on how to approach God, how to talk to Him, and what to ask Him. When we take a wrong step, He is the one who convicts us, helping us realize we have sinned and that we need to repent. As He is doing that,

Christ is interceding for us in heaven before the Father. Remember when Jesus introduced the Holy Spirit as another advocate? That is exactly what He is. He works alongside Christ to make sure that we always have representation before God the Father. His singular goal and purpose is to make sure we are being conformed to the image and likeness of the Son of God. This ought to give us great joy, knowing that we are not being called into a life without help, a life under rules without sympathy and compassion, or a life that is impossible to live in full. The Spirit of God is on a mission to make sure that the work of the cross and the price that was paid for our salvation does not go to waste and that we do not fall back into the condemnation that we were brought out of.

In the American criminal justice system, and in other countries like England, Belgium, and Australia, if a suspect does not have legal representation and cannot afford one, he is assigned what we call a public defender. In America, these are lawyers employed either by the county, the state, or the federal government. Can it be reasonably expected that the public defender will serve a client to the best of his or her ability if the government that employs him or her or that has a contract with the public defender is that same government that is accusing the suspect of a crime? I am not saying a public defender cannot perform an obligation without bias or prejudice, but if everyone had a choice, no one would use a public defender. You'd rather have someone who has no primary connection with the very institution that is trying to put you away, guilty or not.

I am here to tell you that the Holy Spirit is not a public defender. He is not compromised, not working first on your side and then on the side of enemy that wants to put you away. He is not your advocate merely because you cannot afford one; the price for His service has been paid for by the salvation that you have received by faith in Jesus Christ. Since that is the case, He is not here to cut a deal that will save taxpayers the cost of a jury trial. No, He is advocating for what is best for you, to get you off because the price of your sin has been paid by another. He will see that you are declared free and without guilt so you can walk out of that door unashamed and with full confidence to keep living the life God has called you to live. I can go on and on about intercession, but I hope these few words help paint the right picture and help you appreciate the help and support you have in the Holy Spirit.

››› THINK AND TALK ABOUT IT ‹‹‹

Have you ever felt helpless and alone as a child of God? Do you sometimes feel you are cut off from God's grace? Can you think through these experiences to see what revelation or knowledge was missing at the time for you to feel this way, or were there circumstances that made it difficult to believe you have help in the Holy Spirit?

PERFECTION THROUGH PROGRESSION AND PERSEVERANCE

> **So do not throw away your confidence; it will be richly rewarded. You need to persevere so that when you have done the will of God, you will receive what he has promised. For, "In just a little while, he who is coming will come and will not delay." And, "But my righteous one will live by faith. And I take no pleasure in the one who shrinks back." But we do not belong to those who shrink back and are destroyed, but to those who have faith and are saved. (Hebrews 10:35–39)**

If you have been a Christian for a while, you realize that transformation and renewal is a gradual process. There is no one who became a Christian today and who was spotless, sinless, and living in perfection the next day. This raises the question: Should Christians have an expectation that one day they will be without fault and sin in some distant or near future? Or maybe the question to ask is this: Does God expect to look at us and see a life free of sin and guilt, pure and holy without blemish? If the answer to the question is yes, then it may open the door to fear, shame, and discouragement. I'd be hard-pressed to find someone who gave their life to Christ and who has walked sinless since then. On the other hand, if we say the answer to the question is no, then some people unfortunately take that to mean there is license to live in sin and do not even try to walk in the victory of the new life we have been given.

Does God require us to live holy lives? Yes. Does God require us to resist and stay away from sin? Absolutely yes. However, Jesus Christ is presently at the right hand of the Father, ready and willing to make intercession for us when we do fall into sin. It makes one wonder if God knows that our lives will not be perfect or pristine even after we accept Christ as our Lord and Savior. Talking about perfection often leads to endless debates and opinions that I feel become unproductive and offer no meaningful insight to anyone. If that is the case, how do we approach this knowing fully well that we need to understand how to walk with God?

The question I would like to ask is this: Should we even be talking about perfection? My view is that it's a prize or reward at the end of a journey, and what we should really be concerned about is what we need to do to get to the end of that journey so we can claim the reward. If that is the case, we ought to swap the word *perfection* for another word that has more impact on our daily living, and that word is *progression*.

Like newborn babies, crave pure spiritual milk, so that by it you may grow up in your salvation, now that you have tasted that the Lord is good. (1 Peter 2:2–3)

You may put up a good argument on why we can't be perfect, but I doubt if you'd have anything against the need for us to grow as believers. Every newborn baby is expected to grow. At some point, you expect the baby to start making sounds and then ultimately be able to speak. You expect the baby to crawl and then ultimately walk. The baby is expected to progress in these areas and many more. It is the same with our spiritual life as well. We are babies when we become born again. In the passage above, Peter is telling us that we need to grow up in our salvation. He expects that we come to maturity and at some point we stop doing the childish things we were doing at the earlier stage of our born-again lives. There must be movement away from sin and the flesh and toward righteousness and holiness.

Here is an illustration that I love to use: Say sin was a pack of cigarettes, and when you gave your life to Christ you were smoking six packs a week. At some point in your journey, it should hopefully drop to four packs, and then two, and then at a certain point the desire to light one up is not even there. Perhaps this is not exactly how it works, as some people say they lost the desire for sin the moment they gave their lives to Christ. However, I hope it drives home the point that there needs to be progression in the Christian life.

> **For this very reason, make every effort to add to your faith goodness; and to goodness, knowledge; and to knowledge, self-control; and to self-control, perseverance; and to perseverance, godliness; and to godliness, mutual affection; and to mutual affection, love. For if you possess these qualities in increasing measure, they will keep you from being ineffective and unproductive in your knowledge of our Lord Jesus Christ. (2 Peter 1:5–8)**

This is another Scripture passage that highlights the need for progression and growth. Peter is telling us that if the goal is to live productive and effective lives in Christ, then we must do something with our faith. In essence, we can't stay at the same spot as we were when we first gave our lives to Christ. To the faith that we had in Him, the faith that connected us to His salvation, we need to add good works. These works reflect the goodness that God has shown us. But it doesn't stop there; along with these works, we need to increase in our knowledge of God, which means more time studying and meditating on the Word of God and spending time in God's presence. The product of that yields self-control. You must never confuse this to mean that we need to control ourselves with our own power; it simply means that the more we spend time in God's presence and are empowered by His Spirit, the more we graduate to being able to live self-controlled lives, staying away from the things that harm our spirits and grieve God. And we keep going on till we get to love. Peter then talks about having these qualities in increasing measure, which means we keep adding and adding until God comes to get us. This is what the Christian life should be: not stagnant but progressing. Yes, there are days when we take a couple steps back, but the hope is that it does not become a full-on backsliding and degeneration of our lives back into the mess from which we were pulled.

Another word I would like you to take to heart along with *progression* is *perseverance*. The Christian life isn't always going to be good days, and it is very important that we never lose heart or get discouraged if we are not making progress as much as we would want. The ability to get back on the horse after a fall and the ability to stay the course even in the midst of the wind cannot be overemphasized in our daily Christian Walk, especially when we start to look around us and it seems that there is no reward for all this pain and suffering we are putting ourselves through.

Let perseverance finish its work so that you may be mature and complete, not lacking anything. (James 1:4)

Perseverance is what gets us to the finish line, but if we do not let it do its work, then we risk all that work we put in as being a waste, and we will stop growing and increasing in our faith and knowledge of God. It is staying the course that brings maturity. It's progressing daily that brings completeness. If that is the case, then perseverance is much needed.

››› PRAYER OPPORTUNITIES AND FOCUS ‹‹‹

- *Are you able to see contrasts between your life before and after Christ? How measurable is your spiritual growth? Can you evaluate your life without condemning yourself? It is important to do so because this could be a very good fuel for your prayer life.*
- *How is your relationship with the Holy Spirit? Do you know how to access the things we talked about that He provides?*
- *Here are a couple opportunities for prayer:*
    - » *Ask God to search you to see if there are still things that need to change in your life.*
    - » *Ask the Spirit of God for persevering strength and victory over any sin that is troubling your life.*
    - » *Ask God to help you to be confident in and unashamed of your new identity.*

SESSION 4

WHAT KIND OF LIFE IS THIS?

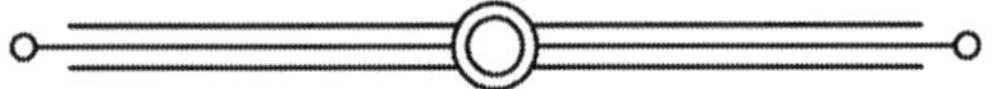

But you have come to Mount Zion, to the city of the living God, the heavenly Jerusalem. You have come to thousands upon thousands of angels in joyful assembly, to the church of the firstborn, whose names are written in heaven. You have come to God, the Judge of all, to the spirits of the righteous made perfect, to Jesus the mediator of a new covenant, and to the sprinkled blood that speaks a better word than the blood of Abel.

(Hebrews 12:22–24)

INTRODUCTION

We have covered a lot of material in the first three sessions of this study, so I would like to use this last session to bring everything together, put things in their proper and right perspective, and most importantly, present the reality of the joy that is experienced with the decision to pursue this life of submission and surrender to God and the acceptance of salvation from His Son, Jesus Christ. We are going to look at ten realities of the Christian life, realities that I believe will help you see the bigger and better picture. Despite the picture the world may paint, despite the misinformation about the Christ-led life, giving your life to Christ is still the best decision you could ever make, and I am a testimony of that. As hard and difficult as the journey may be, no matter the ups and downs, the inconsistencies and chaos, I do not have a single regret. It has given me a way to walk through my earthly life without putting the eternal security of my soul in jeopardy, and I have also experienced and continue to experience the peace, security, joy, and assurance that comes from this life. I can only testify so much; this is a life you will need to experience for yourself. I can assure you that God does not disappoint, He keeps His word and promises, and life will be exactly the way He tells you it will be.

I also hope that all the truth that has been spoken does not discourage you, I understand it is a different message than what is out there, but we do ourselves great harm if all we decide to believe about God is that He is just loving and compassionate to the point that anything goes with Him, that He has no standards to live by, and that He requires nothing from us. Let us not be blinded by the enticement of pleasure, self-satisfaction, and leading our own lives, for it will all come to waste at the end. The Christian life is the only life that will endure, and it is beautiful, purposeful, meaningful, and eternally rewarding, so do not miss out on the great opportunity to experience it.

ICEBREAKER

We love to describe things that we are very proud and joyful about. Can you describe your Christian life with a joy and assurance that encourages others to want to experience the same? You are most likely in a society where this way of life seems foreign and outdated; how could this affect your level of passion about this life? How can one possibly prevent it?

CONVICTION

*For I am not ashamed of the
gospel, because it is the power
of God that brings salvation to
everyone who believes: first to
the Jew, then to the Gentile.*

(Romans 1:16)

What is conviction? Webster's Dictionary says it is the process of being convinced. What then does it mean to be convinced? It is the process of bringing one to a point of belief, consent, or a course of action. Being convicted about the Christian life means you have been brought to the point where you believe that God is the creator of heaven and earth and that He sent His Son to the world to die for your sin and that Jesus rose so you could have a new life. You have also come to believe that the Bible is the eternal Word of God, and that the Gospel is true and powerful. If you look deeper into the dictionary definition, you will see that conviction shows up in belief, in consent, and ultimately in one's course of action. This means that our conviction must be seen in the way we live. We can't say we are Christians if our lives don't reflect our belief. If you believe in something and you are convinced that it is the real thing, then you are not afraid to display it; rather, you wear it proudly and are not bothered about whatever it will cost you.

Conviction does not mean there will not be moments of uncertainty, fear, apprehension, or even at times second thoughts. It is conviction that ultimately brings us back to center, not allowing doubt to derail us or divert our steps. Conviction helps us to hold on to our belief, it sustains us through moments where things may not align with what faith is telling us, it brings comfort and reassurance, and it is ultimately proved true.

Without conviction, we will be tossed back and forth by every wind and wave of ideology and suggestive ways of life, be easily prone to compromise, and be unstable and unreliable to the faith. This is how a lot of us get beaten down when we step into the public sphere, as we are unable to hold on to the core of our belief and faith in God, for whatever reason.

The closer we are to the Word of God, the more we spend time with it and meditate on it, the stronger our conviction will be. This is why it is important for children of God to create time and space to read and study the Word of God, sit with it, ask the Holy Spirit questions, and seek understanding. Some may call this indoctrination, but I call it finding wisdom. The Word of God should be our closest companion and ally.

GRACE

But he said to me, "My grace is sufficient for you, for my power is made perfect in weakness." Therefore I will boast all the more gladly about my weaknesses, so that Christ's power may rest on me.

(2 Corinthians 12:9)

The Christian life is impossible without grace. Trying to live a Christian life without grace is like tying a thousand-pound weight around your ankles and then jumping into the ocean thinking you are going to swim. I don't care how strong you are; you aren't coming back up. Our natural tendency and disposition are sin and rebellion against God, and even though we have the knowledge of good and evil, we do not possess the power over good and evil. When we give our lives to Christ, all the temptations and addictions of our sinful lifestyle don't just disappear or willingly let go of us; they will fight to keep dominance and rule over our lives. It will take the grace of God to start living right and win the battle over sin. Grace is simply power from God to do what He requires of us, knowing fully well we cannot do it ourselves. In this new life, God has guaranteed that we will get all the help that we need to live fulfilled lives. The temptation that was hard to say no to, God gives us grace to overcome. Those addictions that have overpowered and enslaved us, God releases grace to us so we can overcome. In Titus 2:11, Paul says that grace teaches us to say no to unrighteousness, as prior to this, our natural response was yes.

The beautiful thing about grace is that it is always more than the adversity we face, which means we can never run out. In his letter to the Roman church, Paul states that as sin increases, grace increases more. Now, this does not mean that we should go about sinning, thinking that grace will increase and just keep covering us; rather, it is to assure us that even if the devil turns up the heat against us, the grace of God always overwhelms that heat. It will always be sufficient, no matter what situation we find ourselves in.

Grace shows up in our most vulnerable moments, and if your life is anything like mine, that is most of the time. For some reason or the other, we often find ourselves living on the edge, never feeling there is enough strength to move forward, stay righteous, and fulfill His plan for our lives. Moments like these were made for grace to be on full display so that we know to not depend on our own power and ability but always to rely on God. For those who are apprehensive about taking the step of faith into the wonderful life, I would like to announce to you that grace awaits. Don't worry about how you will make it through; what you need to make it through has always been provided and is waiting for you.

MERCY AND FORGIVENESS

For we do not have a high priest who is unable to empathize with our weaknesses, but we have one who has been tempted in every way, just as we are—yet he did not sin. Let us then approach God's throne of grace with confidence, so that we may receive mercy and find grace to help us in our time of need.

(Hebrews 4:15–16)

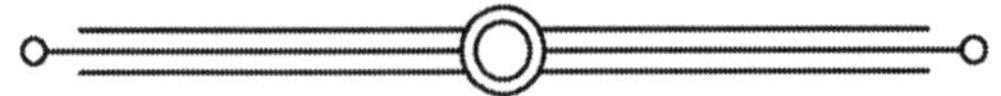

It may sound crazy, but I am always asking God for mercy. I dare say that a good chunk of my prayer time is spent asking God for mercy. Why do I do this? I just don't feel I am ever at a point at which I look at my life and think I have done well enough to deserve or demand anything from God based on how I have lived. I am prone to error, prone to wandering, and even when I find a way to stay out of the major sins, there are still countless ways that I fall short of His expectations.

Mercy is simply not getting the unfavorable treatment you deserve; mercy is when God chooses to forgive your sin and withhold His anger and wrath. That mercy was shown when He hung His Son on the cross, and that mercy is still available after we have given our lives to Him. I often wonder why people run away from God when they sin, and why they keep going further and further into sin until it destroys them. If anything, we need to be running to Him so He can extend His mercy and forgiveness to us. In Psalm 30:5, we are told God's anger lasts only for a moment, but favor takes over from that point. How long or short is a moment? Does it even really matter? What should bring us encouragement is that favor takes over, mercy takes over, and forgiveness is made available.

As much as God hates our sin, He is willing to forgive us when we come to Him in repentance. John, in one of his letters to believers, states that even though his desire is for us to not sin, if we ever get caught up in it, Jesus is faithfully representing and making a case for mercy in God's presence (1 John 2:1). It's an assurance we must constantly remember so the devil does not use the burden of guilt and shame to overwhelm us. Just like the prodigal son, we are never too lost to return, because God's mercy is renewed each day (Lamentations 3:22–23).

It is worth mentioning that the prerequisite for mercy is humility, as no arrogant or proudful person will be able to access God's mercy. We need to understand that the state of our hearts is the most crucial thing when it comes to receiving anything from God. This whole idea of presenting ourselves as victims who deserve to be saved and blessed is just not going to cut it.

POWER AND AUTHORITY

I have given you authority
to trample on snakes and
scorpions and to overcome
all the power of the enemy;
nothing will harm you.

(Luke 10:19)

Something important to note about this newfound life is that you and I will be active participants in what God is doing with us and through us in one capacity or the other. We will not be will-less and speechless, unable to comprehend anything and just being manipulated by a higher spiritual power. On the contrary, we will be empowered to walk this earth representing and reflecting the glory that God has purposed for the earth. We have established that grace comes to us as believers, so this power and authority that we receive is not because we qualified for it but rather because God knows it is something we need to live fulfilled lives, and he also knows that we do not naturally possess it. We will need power to resist temptation and overcome sin, for we must walk the holy walk. God won't do that for us, but He gives us power to do it. We will need power to witness and share the Gospel of salvation and be bold to declare this Gospel in the face of adversity and opposition, being fully aware of the risk of persecution.

Being ambassadors of God's kingdom means we will need to make certain representations, take certain stands, and advocate for things that serve the best interest of the kingdom we belong to. Like an embassy in a foreign nation, the goal of which is to bring awareness to the values and way of life of the country it represents and to make sure that its citizens living in this foreign land are not mistreated in any way, we are authorized to declare and decree God's will and righteousness on this earth. When things are happening around us that do not line up with what God desires, we are authorized to stand in the spiritual gap and, if need be, in the natural gap and come against every spirit and power contrary to His plan. Our authority does not give us the right to be disruptive in society, but it serves as notice to the kingdom of darkness that God is behind us, and we will not be defeated.

Our authority is best reflected when we develop a heart and a passion for God's will to be established in people's lives. We become intercessors, and according to Isaiah 62, we are watchmen who stand on the walls, ready to wage war against spiritual forces and wickedness. If every believer exercised his or her God-given authority, I believe the world would be a much better place right now. It is never too late. God is waiting for us to step into this authority; He has given it to us, and it is ours for the taking.

FREEDOM

It is for freedom that Christ has set us free. Stand firm, then, and do not let yourselves be burdened again by a yoke of slavery. You, my brothers, and sisters, were called to be free. But do not use your freedom to indulge the flesh; rather, serve one another humbly in love.

(Galatians 5:1, 13)

To appreciate the freedom that comes with being born again, one must acknowledge the slavery that sin brings. When we live in sin, I think we are fooled to think that we are in control and that we are doing as we please, but unbeknownst to us, we are under the control of whatever sinful lifestyle we are involved in. We are slaves under sin's system. Then Jesus comes in and frees us from that bondage, removing the power of sin and setting us free. Even after we are forgiven and set free, some of us are still haunted by guilt and shame. We carry around the weight of condemnation. However, the good news is that in Christ, there is freedom from that as well. It does not matter what sinful trail we have left behind because, the power of God's salvation declares we are free and that all charges have been dropped against us. Now that we have been set free from things that ultimately lead to our death and destruction, the question now becomes, What are we now free to do, and is this freedom absolute and without qualification? Look at Paul's speech in his letter to the Roman church.

> **Don't you know that when you offer yourselves to someone as obedient slaves, you are slaves of the one you obey—whether you are slaves to sin, which leads to death, or to obedience, which leads to righteousness? But thanks be to God that, though you used to be slaves to sin, you have come to obey from your heart the pattern of teaching that has now claimed your allegiance. You have been set free from sin and have become slaves to righteousness. (Romans 6:16–18)**

This is very interesting, as what Paul is saying here is that freedom is not really the absence of restraints; rather, it is an opportunity given to live under a set of conditions that results in life, prosperity, and peace and that ultimately glorifies God. In essence, freedom is just slavery under a different system, a righteous and godly system. I know *slavery* is a word that people do not like to hear or be associated with—and for good reason—but if you follow the biblical narrative, slavery started as a voluntary subversion or subjection of oneself under another for the fulfillment of a debt obligation. At some point, man took this to a deviant and depraved level, which should not surprise anyone. The human heart is desperately wicked and outside of God's control; nothing life-giving comes out of it.

SUFFERING AND PERSEVERANCE

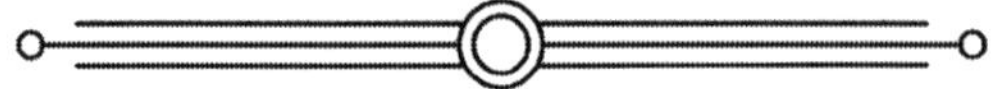

However, if you suffer as a Christian, do not be ashamed, but praise God that you bear that name.

(1 Peter 4:16)

It is possible that we go through suffering and pain for various reasons, but I would like to confine this discussion to the suffering that we have to endure because of our faith. Nowhere in Scripture are we told that accepting Jesus into our lives frees us from trials and tribulations. In fact, Jesus stated that our faith in Him will bring us into contention with the systems of this world. This is the reality of the Christian life, and the earlier we accept this, the better it will be for us because we will avoid being tossed back and forth by false doctrines and falling prey to people who want to manipulate us spiritually. It will also help us to make sure we do not try to force certain things to happen in our lives and in the process compromise our faith and our values.

Suffering because you are a Christian means you will most likely not get the best seat at society's tables, and things will be set up to frustrate your faith in God. You will have to figure out what your priorities are. I see this happen a lot in the creative industry, of which I am a part. I understand that God is a miracle worker, but any Christian artist who thinks they will surpass the fame and popularity of artists who create for sinful indulgence and depravity may find themselves compromising godly standards to make that happen. It's not about skill or ability; it is about the message and what the world wants to consume. In our present society, ungodliness, selfishness, and immorality is what sells. So yes, the platform algorithms will most likely not promote your products as much as you would like, but you must accept that reality. I don't know how a female artist who wants to be godly, is not singing about how good she is in bed, not twerking on stage or in a video, and not being sexually provocative is going to compete with what the world wants her to be. However, she is going to have to be at peace with this and accept this as suffering because of her faith. This is the life we signed up for, and we must be ready to endure the resulting discomfort for our faith in God. I will conclude with the words of the apostle James on this topic:

> **Brothers and sisters, as an example of patience in the face of suffering, take the prophets who spoke in the name of the Lord. As you know, we count as blessed those who have persevered. You have heard of Job's perseverance and have seen what the Lord finally brought about. The Lord is full of compassion and mercy. (James 5:10–11)**

ETERNITY FOCUSED

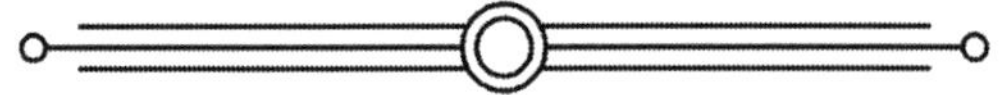

If only for this life we have hope in Christ, we are of all people most to be pitied.

(1 Corinthians 15:19)

To think that Christianity and all that comes with it—coming to repentance, asking for forgiveness, surrendering to Christ, putting in the effort to live in a righteous and holy way, denying oneself and staying away from ungodliness and worldly pleasures—is just for some kind of moral and spiritual status here on earth is simply misguided. Jesus did not sacrifice His life for us just for things to be good here, for us be able to eat well, dress well, drive well, live well, and for all things to be well. The stakes are way bigger than that. The harsh reality of our eternal separation from God is what drove His decision to save us. The moment we become born again, our lives take an eternal approach and focus. Everything is guided by an eternal destination and the desire and hope of having a seat at the heavenly table and a place to call home when this life is done. We receive an assurance that eternity is guaranteed for us, the blessings we receive are spiritual, and every seed of righteousness sown in us is a deposit guaranteeing that eternity.

Some people do not believe there is a life after this earthly one, and it makes it easy for them to live however they like and on their own terms. They make decisions on impulse with self at the forefront, without a thought of any eternal consequence whatsoever. We believe differently because we know differently, and we have experienced differently. Jesus Himself told us directly and through many of His parables that this life is not all there is; there is more to life than this temporal existence that will pass, whether it be when He comes or when this earthly suit expires and the spirit returns to the Creator to give an account and receive a due reward. With this in mind, we approach our daily lives not as foolish but wise, understanding that our days are short and the days are evil, and the only hope of escaping the evil and inevitable destruction is the hope we have in Christ.

Do not let your hearts be troubled. You believe in God; believe also in me. My Father's house has many rooms; if that were not so, would I have told you that I am going there to prepare a place for you? And if I go and prepare a place for you, I will come back and take you to be with me that you also may be where I am. (John 14:1–3)

GRATITUDE AND WORSHIP

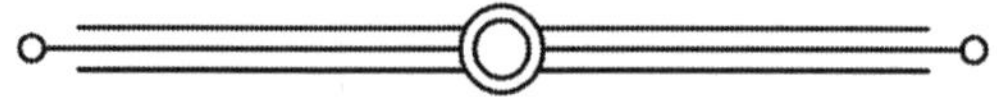

Therefore, I urge you, brothers and sisters, in view of God's mercy, to offer your bodies as a living sacrifice, holy and pleasing to God—this is your true and proper worship.

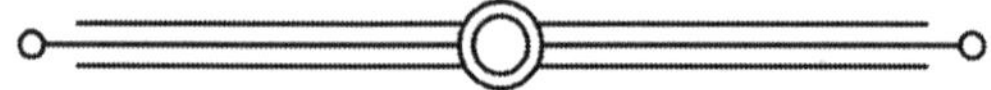

If every morning when we wake up, we remember that the life we live is privileged, then we will always be in a state of gratitude to God for everything. I speak first from a spiritual perspective. When we understand that the penalty for our past has been taken away and that even our present errors find forgiveness by His blood, if we understand that our justification is from someone else's sacrifice and that love drove that sacrifice, then we ought to live lives that reflect gratitude.

The beauty of having a relationship with God is that the closer we get to Him, the more we see who He really is and the more we experience His value and worth. Relating to Him based on this revelation means that we acknowledge and ascribe this worth back to Him through how we live. Worship is not the song that we sing; it's not the concerts we go to and the records we listen to. It is the state and the stage of life that expresses gratitude and ascribes worth by offering what is most valuable to it in response to what it has received. Simply put, worshiping God is letting Him have our lives the same way He gave us His. This is what makes those other things that we do and call worship meaningful or not. God is interested not only in the voice but in the vessel as well. If the vessel is not worshiping, the voice is simply singing. If the vessel is not worshiping, the hands have simply been raised in vain, and we are at best attendees in any church service or concert.

It is hard to be a Christian and be arrogant at the same time. It just does not add up. To have a sense of entitlement and pride about life will make it impossible to live a life of gratitude and worship. To feel that every blessing that has come your way, every door of opportunity that has opened, every breakthrough you've gotten, every act of kindness and mercy is because you somehow deserve it is as arrogant as it gets. This not what God recommends for us, His children. We ought to live in humility, knowing that God did not have to do all that He did, and we should be constantly thankful not only in words but in the way we live.

> **Praise the Lord, my soul; all my inmost being, praise his holy name. Praise the Lord, my soul, and forget not all his benefits—who forgives all your sins and heals all your diseases, who redeems your life from the pit and crowns you with love and compassion, who satisfies your desires with good things so that your youth is renewed like the eagle's. (Psalm 103:1–5)**

HOLINESS

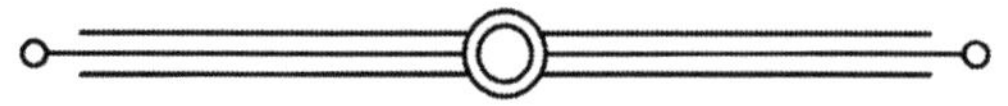

But just as he who called you is holy, so be holy in all you do; for it is written: "Be holy, because I am holy."

(1 Peter 1:15–16)

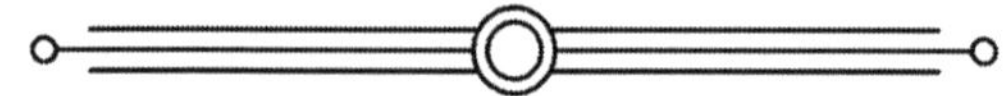

I said it before, and I'll say it again: sin is the reason Jesus came. Sin and death are what He battled against and was victorious over. Since this is the case, the victory we speak of will be judged on what sin is able to do to us after we have claimed this victory. With the power we have received, we should be able to resist the temptation and the allure of sin. I of all people understand that we are constantly tripping and erring but let us not be confused. It is not because there is no power over the sin with which we are struggling; rather, it is because we end up giving in to our sinful and selfish desires. The hope is that the more time we spend with God, the more we realize that there is power and grace to overcome whatever sin we struggle with, and we determine to let that grace work in us and through so that our victory becomes obvious and apparent. The Christian life requires holiness and godliness, and God is ready to work with us daily to ensure that we live life accordingly.

Dear children, do not let anyone lead you astray. The one who does what is right is righteous, just as he is righteous. The one who does what is sinful is of the devil, because the devil has been sinning from the beginning. The reason the Son of God appeared was to destroy the devil's work. No one who is born of God will continue to sin, because God's seed remains in them; they cannot go on sinning, because they have been born of God. (1 John 3:7–9)

At some point, there will be no excuse. We must allow the grace of God to lead us away from sin and foolishness and to the path of wisdom and holiness. We can't keep making excuses or even keep thinking that living in sin does not matter just because forgiveness is available. That never ends well.

The devil knows that if he can keep us in the sin cycle, he can disrupt our relationship with God. I think people fail to realize that the devil is doomed as he is. However, he understands exactly what is at stake and what he is doing. This is not someone just throwing tantrums and being mad about what will become of him. He knows God enough to know that the one thing that can keep anyone out of His eternal presence is sin. Therefore, until God brings everything to an end, he will continue working to ensnare us with sin so that we also miss out on eternity with God, just as he is already condemned to be.

PRAYER

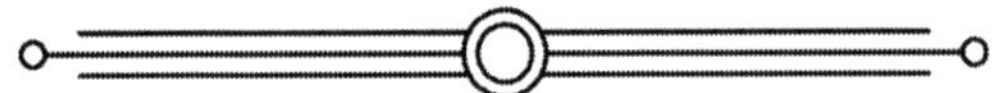

Devote yourselves to prayer,
being watchful and thankful.

(Colossians 4:2)

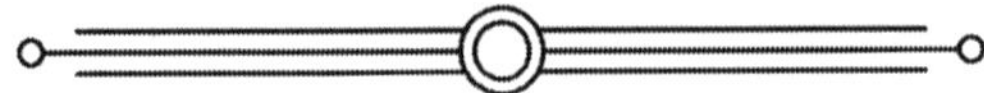

Let us not make a mystery of this. Prayer is simply communication with God, but as simple as this may sound, this is the one thing that quite a lot of believers often trip on by either not really understanding the importance of it or using it for the wrong things. Let me start by first saying it is impossible to grow in a relationship and enter more intimate phases if there is no communication, and not only communication, but two-way communication. Unfortunately, it seems to be that in these times, God is the only one doing the talking. Not a lot of Christians take prayer seriously, or they feel that they do not have to invest adequate time and effort in this area.

Second, I often hear people say that if all you have is five minutes to talk to God in a day, that is good enough. I hate to break it to you, but this is the most ridiculous advice. I would advise you to throw it out like garbage, because between you and me, if we are honest with ourselves, you have more than five minutes. I know they say this to mean that little time is better than no time, but it is still wrong advice to give. I do not assume that folks are just sitting around and doing nothing with their lives, but I would like to know how busy life is for God to only get five minutes or fragments of whatever remains of the day. I don't know how long you should pray, but I know you should make prayer a priority. Whatever is your priority takes precedence, and if prayer comes after everything else, then it means it is not a priority.

I acknowledge that because it is also a spiritual act, there are additional layers of struggle, but we don't solve that problem by giving in to the struggle; rather, we ask God for grace to overcome it. There have been days when I started my day or got out of the house without praying, and I'd pray in the car on the way to wherever I am going, but I would hope this does not happen seven days in a week or even every four or three. If it does, then something needs to be addressed. It is all about what we prioritize and, if need be, sacrifice for. We are talking about God here, the one we sing about and tell the whole world about how much He loves us and how we love Him. If that is really the case, He should not be the last on our list—He should be first.

Without prayer, it is impossible to be empowered as a child of God. The devil knows that if he can keep us prayerless, he can keep us powerless. We must make it a duty to go into God's presence, seek His face, spend time in His Word, and pray about what we are reading. If you spend time asking for His will to be done, lay aside everything else, create a moment and space that nothing else matters but your time with Him, then I guarantee that you will see the benefits of this in your life, and you will be more confident in Him, especially during trying and chaotic times.

Then he returned to his disciples and found them sleeping. "Couldn't you men keep watch with me for one hour?" he asked Peter. "Watch and pray so that you will not fall into temptation. The spirit is willing, but the flesh is weak." (Matthew 26:40–41)

››› PRAYER OPPORTUNITIES AND FOCUS ‹‹‹

- *Do you ever wonder about this life that God has called us to live? Do you ever have doubts about anything and everything? Doubts present opportunities to have conversations with God. If this is you, take the opportunity and lay it at God's feet in the place of prayer. Our God is a reassuring God.*

- *As an exercise, can you contrast some or all of the things we talked about with the world's understanding of the Christian life?*
- *If you have not come to terms with what life will be as a born-again child of God, are you able to identify why?*

FINAL THOUGHTS

This is not all there is to say, but this discussion is enough to stir up the need to pursue Christ and His righteousness, stir up passion and the desire to know God better, and begin the journey of securing eternity. The message of the cross is not confusing, as some have claimed it to be. God is clear in His offering and instructions. To the one who will open his or her heart to receive, it is not complicated at all. But to those who turn away, harden their hearts, and refuse to believe, the message of the cross will forever seem foolish.

But in case you did not catch the whole point of this book, here is a recap of all that has been said. We really don't have power over our lives, a man who did not determine the day of his birth and cannot control the day he exits this life should be very careful as to how he defines the freedom he thinks he has. Everything is a privilege, and understanding this helps us to stay humble and acknowledge that without salvation, we are headed the wrong way. God does not force salvation on anyone, nor does He trick us to be saved or bribe us with wealth and riches. Every one of us will have to make this decision to turn our lives over to Him. Not only that, but we also must decide in our hearts to live our lives in His presence daily. No one said it would be easy. The Christian life is a blessed life, but it is a challenging one as well, and it can sometimes be a very rough ride. There is hope, however: there is grace that has been promised, there is help every step of the way, and God will never put more on us than we can bear. We need to be encouraged and not let all the crazy things happening in the world make us renounce our faith in Him. It is rough out here in the streets. There is so much vying for our attention, calling us to come have fun, to seek pleasure without restraint, to be self-indulgent, self-leading, and arrogant. We need to make sure our desires don't lead us on a path of self-destruction while being fooled into thinking that sin no longer has an impact on our relationship with God.

If you have not made the decision to accept Jesus Christ into your life, I encourage you to do so today. You need God—we all need Him. A life outside of Christ is a life that is lived and will end in eternal darkness. It does not matter the sin, dysfunction, and the chaos of the moment; this is exactly what Jesus came for: to save those who are lost. It is a simple but profound confession: "Jesus, I acknowledge that I am a sinner. I ask that You forgive my sins, and I invite You to be my Lord and Savior." If you pray that prayer, God will take it from there.

I would also like to encourage you not to do Christianity alone. The devil knows how to use isolation to lure us away from believing the truth. As hard as it is becoming to find a very good Bible-based church, a church that still holds on to the integrity of the Word of God and has not joined the secularist groups, there are still churches and fellowships out there that you can be a part of and where you can grow with other believers. One must prayerfully approach the search and believe that God will never lead you astray. Make sure your circle of friends are people who are also growing in the faith. This is not to say that you will not have relationships with people who either do not believe or are still on the fence about it, but when it comes to core relationships, it is better to have people who hold the same values as you, so that your approach to how you handle life will stem from the same foundation.

Observe your life, and make notes of your growth and struggles, your high and low points as you walk in Christ. These are what make up the substance in your prayer life: showing gratitude and pouring out worship to God and reaching out for grace to help you in time of need. The impact of God's salvation on your life starts the minute you say yes to Him. We are looking forward to being where He is when this life is over, but the victory Christ won on the cross is also for the present. It is for us to live victorious lives here on earth.

Stay close to the Word of God. As God instructed Joshua, daily meditation is the key to understanding and growth. When people ask if the Bible has all the answers to life's questions, I say the Bible has everything you need to live. Open it up and become a student of it, and you will realize that it will lead you and guide you to God's plan and purpose for your life. The more you read, the more you understand, and the more you understand, the more you are able to stand up and defend the faith that you profess, not in arrogance but in humility and reverence.

Most importantly, salvation may be free to you, but it came at a cost to someone. Do not belong to the group of people who abuse this great gift. Everyone will give an account of how they lived; those who received this salvation will give an account of what they did with the seed. Hopefully our account will be that we added to this gift of righteousness, goodness; and to goodness, knowledge; and to knowledge, self-control; and to self-control, perseverance; and to perseverance, godliness; and to godliness, mutual affection; and to mutual affection, love. These were the words of Peter in his second letter (2 Peter 1:5–7). Don't join the group of Christians who say, "Once saved, forever saved; therefore, I can do whatever I like." I can promise you that it will not end well for them if they continue on this path. As for you, keep the faith and make your way to the end, where God is waiting with open arms to receive you into the inheritance that He has ready for those who believe to the end.

I leave you with the word of the apostle John, a statement he made regarding his testimony about all that Jesus did while on earth. My prayer is that you will heed that encouragement and choose to believe.

> **Jesus performed many other signs in the presence of his disciples, which are not recorded in this book. But these are written that you may believe that Jesus is the Messiah, the Son of God, and that by believing you may have life in his name. (John 20:30–31)**

ACKNOWLEDGMENTS

Writing a book will always be a humbling experience for me, especially a book that talks about the Christian faith. For God to entrust me with knowledge and revelation, without which this book would have been impossible to finish, I express my profound gratitude to Him. When I started writing this book, I did not have the faintest idea how it would come together, but I realized that every moment that I obeyed the Spirit of God and got in front of the computer, my were eyes were opened to His truth. I am thankful that He led me, and I am a living testimony of His goodness and kindness.

Thanks also go to my wife, Ola, for always standing by me and loving me. She has been a source of strength and encouragement over the years, and I love her dearly. My two wonderful daughters, Gabrielle and Danielle, are two of a kind, and I owe them a great deal of thanks as well. They've grown to be very dedicated and committed children, and it affords me a great deal of time to commit to projects like this. I'd also like to thank my siblings, Comfort, Biola, Buki, and Rotimi, for their love and support over the years, for all the childhood memories and for doing life together. I owe my parents, Simeon and Lydia, a great deal of gratitude for the way we were raised. The love and discipline they gave us has been very instrumental in my life.

I belong to a very vibrant Bible-based church, Grace Community Church in Fulton, Maryland, and being a member of this church has been very fulfilling. I've come to know some very wonderful people and have been encouraged by how people have dedicated their lives to loving God and serving Him. I am very grateful for our lead pastor, Mitchell Lee, for all the teaching, guidance, and encouragement, both in and out of the pulpit. I am thankful for the other pastors as well, who graciously and gladly serve in the house and are diligent in their love and affection for the church.

I can't forget to mention the worship team of which my wife and I are a part. It is such a beautiful group with beautiful people. Special thanks to Christine, our worship director, for her dedication to making sure everything is ready for us, as well as her openness and transparency. This has made serving in the worship team a fun and fulfilling experience.

To everyone who has had an impact in my life, I am thankful, and you're always in my heart. I pray that God's grace will find you wherever you are, that His peace will always be with you, and most importantly, that your soul will make nowhere else a resting place but the saving arms of Christ, who offers redemption and the promise of eternity for all those who put their trust in Him.

Made in the USA
Middletown, DE
03 April 2025

73745046R00095